TRIATHLONS
FOR WOMEN

SALLY EDWARDS

FOREWORD BY KAREN SMYERS

TRIATHLONS
FOR WOMEN

THIRD EDITION

VELO press

BOULDER, COLORADO

TRAINING PLANS, EQUIPMENT, NUTRITION

Printed in the United States of America.

13 12 11

Distributed in the United States and Canada by Publishers Group West.

Library of Congress Cataloging in Publication Data

Edwards, Sally, 1947–
    Triathlons for women / Sally Edwards. — 3rd ed.
        p. cm.
    Includes bibliographical references (p.) and index.
    ISBN 978-1-931382-05-2
        1. Triathlon—Training—Handbooks, manuals, etc. I. Title: Triathlons. II. Title.

GV1060.73 .E395 2002
796.42'57—dc21

2002066354

Cover photo by Galen Nathanson.

VeloPress
1830 N. 55th Street
Boulder, CO 80301-2700 USA
303/440-0601; Fax 303/444-6788; E-mail velopress@insideinc.com;
Web velopress.com

CONTENTS

Foreword

First, allow me to say how excited I am you are reading Sally Edwards's *Triathlons for Women*. If you are reading this book, you are either taking the first step toward becoming a triathlete or improving your race performance. Like Sally, I have been competing in triathlons for several years. Both of us started racing in triathlons because they are fun and challenging, and then we ended up making our careers in the sport: I am a professional triathlete, and Sally is an athlete, coach, writer, motivator, and spokesperson for the Danskin Triathlon Series. Like Sally, I am passionate about encouraging more women to discover their inner athlete and to "try a 'tri.' "

When I first started participating in triathlons in 1984, there were very few sources of information on the sport. Like most triathletes, I learned things the hard way—through trial and error. All on my own, I discovered what not to eat the morning of the race, how to lose your bike in the transition area, and how much training before a race is too much training. Luckily, everything you need to know about training for and racing in a triathlon is now in this informative and inspiring book, *Triathlons for Women.*

There is no question that entering your first triathlon can be intimidating. Because of the three-sport format, it is as if there are three times as many questions. Glancing around before the start of a race, it may appear everyone else is a seasoned, extremely fit veteran with the most expensive high-tech equipment available; however, if you look closely at the transition area of your local triathlon, you will find equipment ranging from mountain bikes to touring bikes to the latest racing bikes. And while you also will see a wide range of body types and levels of fitness, every woman will have the same gleam in her eye, reflecting the determination to meet her personal goals.

You will discover that your feelings of intimidation are unfounded when you do your first race. There tends to be a lot of camaraderie in triathlon, especially in the all-women races. One of my fondest memories during my eighteen years of racing is from my first all-women's race. As I was leading the charge on the last mile of the out-and-back 5K run, many of the other women were just starting their run as we crossed paths. Every single woman cheered for me as I went by. When I finished, I went back to the course, as did most of the top women, and returned the favor by encouraging the women who were still racing. Although each woman was focused on achieving her own goal, each still had the energy and awareness to support every other competitor in the race. It was an incredibly positive and motivating atmosphere in which to compete.

When I attended the pre-race meeting for first-time triathletes at a Danskin race in Boston, I listened to Sally, one of the best motivational speakers I have ever heard, completely enthrall a very nervous bunch of women. Step-by-step, she took them through everything they could expect to encounter during the race. At the same time, she inspired feelings of confidence and empowerment to such degrees that they were palpable. She made every one of those women believe in herself and her goal, and at the same time laugh at her jokes, which made the tension just melt away. I wanted to turn back the clock and become one of those first-timers, because I envied their sense of anticipation and the feeling of accomplishment they were going to experience the next day.

Sally's dedication to making the Danskin Triathlon Series a success is evidenced by her participation in the race. Sally swims, bikes, and runs with the last woman in the race, giving her constant encouragement and positive reinforcement, and saving every woman from the most prevalent first-timer worry: finishing last. Sally gladly accepts the last-place position and in turn does every woman in the race the favor of removing that anxiety.

Sally drew on her vast experience in the sport of triathlon to write this book. Her insight into which questions people need answered, her ability to explain the basics of swimming, biking, and running in an understandable way for novice and experienced racers alike, and the inspiration she provides along the way are what make this third edition of *Triathlons for Women* so indispensable. With this book, you are armed with all the information you need to train for and compete in a triathlon. Now go forth and "tri" your best!

KAREN SMYERS
Seven-time National Champion (1990–1995, 2001)
Hawaiian Ironman Champion (1995)
ITU World Triathlon Champion (1990, 1995)

Acknowledgments

I would like to acknowledge how this twenty-first century revision came to life. In the early 1990s, I wrote a triathlon book series of three titles all published by a major triathlon magazine: *Triathlons for Fun, Triathlons for Women,* and the third in the trilogy, *Triathlons for Kids.* That was in the last century. It's now ten years later and time to update and revise the books to make them current and more applicable. The first step was to form a team of individuals who could make that happen. In doing so, I first selected two triathletes—Rebecca Yao and Kaari Busick—who are experts in the art of writing and are both excellent age group triathletes. I want to thank them for the quality of their work in revising and editing the text. I truly want to thank them for their contribution and the joy I had working with them both.

But Rebecca Yao and Kaari Busick (Bellevue, Washington) are more than triathletes and writers. They both worked tirelessly to make this book bigger and better. I can never thank them enough. Also, their contributions to the sport of triathlon deserve special attention. Rebecca serves as the National Coordinator of the Danskin Mentor-Mentee program. She donates hundreds of hours a year to run a program that teaches women how to mentor using sports as the platform. Together, they connect thousands of new triathletes with experienced triathletes to help each have a more positive and successful triathlon experience.

Second, after more than a dozen Ironman triathlon races and over eighty Danskin race finishes, I owe a great tribute to the sport of triathlon and all of the organizations and individuals who have made it grow over the past thirty years. As one of the early pioneers of triathlon in the United States, I know that many gave enormously to see that the opportunity exists for nearly every individual to participate.

Finally, in all reality, this book owes a great deal to the individuals who are responsible for executing the Danskin Women's Triathlon Series. In particular, thanks go to the company Danskin Inc. for ownership and production of the most successful and oldest triathlon series in the world. Thanks to Maggie Sullivan, Danskin's Vice President and Series Director, for her role in throwing the wonderful party known as the Danskin Women's Triathlon Series that has served as the entry point into a new way of living for so many of us. Launched by Danskin's President, Greg Rorke, in 1990, the Danskin Women's Triathlon has been my passion for the past thirteen years, and I have served as its national spokesperson. Danskin has now provided an opportunity for nearly 100,000 women to finish their first triathlon and to realize nearly 100,000 dreams that took each of those caterpillars to crossing the finish line like a butterfly.

When was the last time you did something for the first time? This is a question that deserves your own personal answer. I hope reading this book, learning more about training, setting and accomplishing goals, and the process of living the healthy lifestyle of a triathlete will be but one answer to that question. From my heart, thanks to all of you.

SALLY EDWARDS
Member, Triathlon Hall of Fame
National Spokesperson, Danskin Women's Triathlon Series since 1990
80-Time Danskin Triathlon Finisher and 16-Time Ironman Finisher
Author
The Head Heart, Heart Zones, a Training and Education Company
Keynote Speaker

Sally Edwards running on the Great Wall of China.

WOMEN AS ATHLETES

From Tomboy to Athlete

Our fathers are proud. Our mothers are amazed. We're winning races, finishing marathons, training for triathlons, swimming before work, and touring on our bikes rather than in our cars.

This is the twenty-first century, and women are into sports. There are more women in sports today than at any other time in history, and we are feeling the effects—the enhanced self-esteem, the feelings of achievement, and the joy of excellence. What took us so long?

At the 1990 Danskin Women's Triathlon Series in Long Beach, these feelings were alive. As the men stood on the sidelines as support crew and the women competed, there was a feeling of exhilaration and energy in the air. And at the awards ceremony, it was a man who pointed out just how much the basic attitudes about female athletes have changed. In explaining the newfound and hard-fought acceptance of women as athletes, then-president of the 108-year-old Danskin company, Greg Rorke, said to the hundreds in the audience, "A generation ago you would have been labeled tomboys.

*Let her
Swim,
Climb mountain peaks,
Pilot airplanes,
Battle against the elements,
Take risks,
Go out for adventure,
And
She will not
Fell before the world
… timidity.*
—**Simone de Beauvoir**

You know, women who want to be like men, or girls who want to be like boys. But, you also know that girls love sports the same way that boys do. You are each athletes, not tomboys."

Greg was right. Here was a group of female athletes that several decades ago would have been labeled with the same social stigma that was applied to me: I was raised a "tomboy."

Today we are raising our children as girl and women athletes, not as tomboys. The derogatory label has been dropped, and a whole generation of girls is growing up with a vision of themselves as strong, competent, and capable of anything.

That's what I want for each of us, and that's part of what I think triathlon provides.

The History of Women in Triathlons

Though triathlon has a short history, it is full of colorful tales that capture the imagination and the spirit of sport.

Races such as the Ironman are the best example. In my second Ironman competition, as an Ironwoman, I shared a memorable finish-line experience. The year before, in 1981, I had finished second in what is now considered a slow 12 hours and 37 minutes, and a woman named Lyn Brooks had taken third place. In 1982 I knew that she was ahead of me as I started to run the marathon, and I knew that running was her first sport, as it was mine.

After nine hours spent swimming 2.4 miles and cycling 112 miles, at the five-mile point in the marathon, I caught Lyn. We were both exhausted and reduced to running a fatigue-laden, eight-and-a-half-minute-per-mile pace, so we shuffled along, side by side. It was the first time we had met—we knew of each other only by reputation.

Neither of us had the energy left to compete, so I asked Lyn if she would like to run those last few miles together and tie. Without pause, she agreed, and a wave of relief passed over me. I'll never forget those last few miles together running, sweating, and frying under the Hawaiian sun that gave no mercy. That day Lyn and I shared something that is difficult to find in most places in life—the mutual respect, trust, and love that athletes experience when they have given their all in pursuit of self-accomplishment and the finish line.

We ended up tying for third, with a final time of 11 hours and 51 minutes, almost one hour faster than our times had been the year before. In fact, our 1982 time was fast enough to have won the 1981 race. Lyn and I were obviously not the only ones who were improving their times.

Indeed, the toppling of finish-time records in women's triathlon has been a consistent phenomenon, and we have come a long way very quickly. When Paula Newby-Fraser broke the course record with a 9:01 in 1988, few ignored the fact that no man had broken 9:01 before 1983. And, with each passing year, the times continue to drop.

Triathlon stands out in the history of sports, since from its inception female triathletes have been accepted as bona fide competitors, not as a sideshow to the main event. Compare this with track, where women were barred from competing in anything longer than 200 meters until the 1960 Olympic Games, because the International Olympic Commission decreed that greater distances were too strenuous for the female constitution. The women's 3,000-meter run wasn't even added to the Olympics until 1984, the same year the women's marathon was first included as an Olympic sport. Finally, triathlon is an Olympic event, and women's triathlon was the opening event for the 2000 Olympics in Sydney, Australia.

From triathlon's beginnings, women have been in for the duration—the long haul and even the hard crawl.

There were two Ironman races in 1982, one in February and another in October, as the race was officially repositioned as a fall event. The February race was especially memorable, because after suffering from severe dehydration and exhaustion, Julie Moss crumpled to the ground fifteen yards from the finish line, and moments before she crossed on her hands and knees, Kathleen McCartney passed her for the first-place victory. ABC television captured the moment and televised it across the world as one of the most heroic finishes ever in the history of sports. Many current Ironpeople have said that watching Julie crawl those last yards so inspired them that they decided to take up the sport. In 1987 the scene was replayed as Jan Ripple crawled across the finish line, suffering in the same way, and an amazing moment of combined abasement and victory was again presented to the world.

Women have played other roles in triathlon than that of athlete, having been central in the leadership of the sport from its beginnings. Pioneers such as Lyn Brooks and I volunteered endless hours organizing the Triathlon Federation USA, America's national governing body of triathlon. Internationally, Sarah Springman served in a similar role, working to develop and enhance the position of women in the European arena.

Directorship in the sport has also been a woman's role. The Ironman had a woman, Valerie Silk, at its helm for over a decade. Silk brought ABC's *Wide World of Sports,* prize money, and an international circuit to the event that she founded, owned, and later sold. Sponsorships, too, have been cultivated by women. The Budweiser brewing company's sponsorship, the key source of capital in triathlon's formative years, was orchestrated by Jane Marks, whose vision of aligning a beer product with a lifestyle sport was squarely on the mark.

On the technical side, the first computerized timing program, which produces split times (including transition times), was developed by Bonnie Miller (Joseph) in 1982.

Clearly, a woman's place in triathlon is in the race—whether as a triathlete, organizer, director, or engineer.

Triathlon has rapidly expanded in America, with women-only events emerging as a well-respected tradition. A women-only triathlon was first held at Marine World Africa USA in 1982, sponsored by Bonne Bell, the skin care and cosmetics company that also sponsored a national 10K running series. In 1990 Danskin, the women's dancewear company, introduced new lines of broad-spectrum women's athletic apparel and sponsored a three-city national triathlon series. By 2000, the Danskin Women's Triathlon Series had expanded to cover seven cities and is now the premier women-only multisport series with nearly 100,000 women finishers.

Triathlon in Europe has grown in a fashion similar to the U.S. pattern. According to European multitriathlon champion Sarah Springman, a professional triathlete with a doctoral degree in engineering who teaches now in Switzerland, "Triathlon arrived in Europe in 1982 with the first Nice Triathlon." By 1984, Springman and her all-female team were competing in the London-to-Paris Triathlon (which consisted of a swim across the English Channel, individual 30-mile cycling time trials, a 50-mile team time trial to Paris, and a marathon run by a relay team of four). Finishing in tenth place out of sixteen mostly male teams, Ironwoman Springman says the outcome "rearranged some male egos and impressions of triathlon women."

At the pre-race party several nights before the 1998 Ironman, the master of ceremonies honored all those who were seasoned triathletes, as is his tradition. He asked everyone who had finished the Hawaii event five times or more to stand. Hundreds of the 1,500 entrants stood. Then, slowly, he asked everyone to sit who had not finished the race six times. Dozens lowered themselves into their chairs. Next, he asked those who hadn't finished seven times, then eight, then nine, then ten times, then 11, 12, 13, 14, 15, 16, 17, 18 times to sit down.

In 1998 two individuals were left standing—1982 Ironman champion Scott Tinley and Lyn Brooks.

He then asked anyone who had not finished nineteen times to sit.

Scott sat. Lyn stood.

After two decades of never missing an Ironman, the woman who tied with me for third place is still racing what is considered one of the toughest races in the world. In 1999 she finished her twentieth consecutive Ironman. Race management gave her a new Isuzu for her accomplishment. She said it was her last year.

Both she and Scott again finished. Lyn was the solitary figure left standing at the end of this rite, in an audience of thousands, in an event that circles the globe, in a race that compares to no other.

The Five Answers to the Five Basic Questions

1. WHO? Who should participate in this triple-fitness sport?

Answer: Anyone who wants to.

If you don't want to, then don't. But if you want to have some fun, get fit, and meet some new people who are interested in the same kinds of things, then triathlons might be just right for you.

2. HOW? How do I start, and how do I keep it all together and not quit?

Answer: It won't be easy, but it's doable.

You've taken a right step by reading this book, and if you start to slide back, pick up the book again and reread it; I wrote it to motivate you. This is your life, and this is your agenda—it's not like starting a diet or a car. Starting a diet only leads to failure, because in the long run you only change what you eat, not what you do. It's also not like starting a car, where all you do is slide in the ignition key and stomp on the gas pedal. Triathlon, if you do it right, is a lifetime fitness program and a serious and rewarding commitment of will.

3. WHEN? When can I find time for all of this training when I'm already busy?

Answer: If there's a will, there's time. Prioritize and organize your time according to your beliefs and goals.

You aren't reading this book or training for triathlons because you are bored or because there is nothing else to do in your life. You are probably reading it because you want more: more challenges, more information, more motivation. If there is a place for fitness in your life, there is time for tri-training. It isn't easy, and you may have to make some trade-offs. But when you make your health your first priority and when you know that being physically fit is the foundation of your health, training becomes important enough to make time for.

Most people see tri-training as impossible because they think it's so time-consuming and strenuous. They're wrong. When you make the transition from your current workout program, there will be no greater time requirements than you have already. Designing a swim-bike-run training program not only can be more fun and challenging, but it needn't cost you any additional time. If you don't believe me, skip ahead and read the chapters on training.

4. WHERE? Where do I train, meet people, learn more, and so on?
Answer: The answers to these questions are all around you.

Network through your local resources. In most communities there are bike, swim, run, and triathlon retail stores that can connect you with people. There are sports clubs—Y's, athletic clubs, and health clubs—that you can join. There are organizations like the Danskin Mentor-Mentee program and magazines available to you. The network is already there—join it. And you can always contact me; drop an e-mail to staff@heartzone.com.

5. WHAT? What do I have to do to compete in and complete a triathlon?
Answer: You must combine the three components of athletic success: efficient biomechanics (how your body moves), proper equipment, and a training plan.

In the following sections, each of the three triathletic sports—swim, bike, and run—is presented along with its components, in order for you to build a solid triathletic foundation that will support you through training, competition, and a lifetime of fitness.

All the joy of triathlons is waiting for you—come and get it!

HEART ZONES TRAINING

Why a Heart Rate Monitor

Fifteen years ago when I purchased my first one, heart rate monitors (HRMs) cost in the $500 price range. Today they cost as little as $40 to $50—less than the price of a pair of good workout shoes. Monitors are readily available in athletic clubs, sporting goods stores, on websites, and through direct mail. HRMs once were only part of the professional athlete's world. Now heart rate monitors and heart rate training enable people of every fitness level to monitor their effort and get the most out of their training time.

Training for a triathlon must fit you as an individual. We only have so much time to train, and that time must be spread among three separate sports —swimming, biking, and running. A heart rate monitor is the great equalizer in a multisport program. It gives you a precise way to determine how hard your swim, bike, and run workouts should be in any given week or month. Heart rate monitor training (known today as heart zones training) gets the results you want over time. You won't spend too much time or intensity in one sport to the detriment of others. I'm convinced, and so are thousands of professional and amateur triathletes alike who train using this technological approach, that it will lead to the integration of your mind, your body, and your spirit into a triathlon training program that works for you long-term.

Estelle Gray, co-owner of R&E Cycles in Seattle, Washington, training and riding with her best friend, a heart rate monitor.

I know that if you've picked up this book, you are looking for the best in yourself. If you don't have an HRM, put down this book and go buy the best one you can afford. More money means more features. Period. I'll meet you back here.

If you are still reading and don't have your heart rate monitor (yet), I'm including this chart here so you can see the correlation of your subjective rate of perceived exertion to heart rate zones. Perceived exertion is based on your subjective feeling of the exercise intensity, a holdover from the 1950s. Perceived exertion is the method used when exercise research was in its infancy. Today, we have better tools and information in the form of a personal power tool, the HRM. Again, I encourage you to take the leap and begin using one.

PERCEIVED EXERTION TABLE			
Zone	Percent of Maximum Heart Rate	Rate of Perceived Exertion	Description of the Feeling
5	90–100	9–10	Extremely hard to maximal
4	80–90	7–8	Very, very hard
3	70–80	5–6	Hard!
2	60–70	3–4	Moderate to somewhat hard
1	50–60	1–2	Very light, easy

Determining Your Max HR

By definition, maximum heart rate (max HR) is the fastest your body will let your heart contract within a one-minute period. The newest information has shown that everyone's maximum heart rate is different and not age-dependent (as previously believed and used as the basis for old heart rate charts). A maximal stress test and health appraisal by a physician or sports physiologist is the safest and most recommended way to determine your precise max HR. There are many other ways to estimate your max HR; here are two (remember, there may be some error to these methods, since they are estimates):

1. If you have a heart rate monitor and have worn it quite a while, simply use the largest number you have seen on the monitor (assuming you have done some hard workouts or races) for each of the sporting activities in which you participate. Max HR will be slightly different for each sport.

2. Enter a 5K running race, and during the last one to two minutes go to a full sprint. Add five beats to the highest number recorded on the monitor during this time period.

If you aren't in shape and haven't been for a while, you should not take a test designed to bring you to your actual maximum heart rate. Remember, if you have any questions about your health, consult a physician before engaging in vigorous physical activity.

What's in a Number?

If you are just beginning to return to fitness, it's fine to use one of the techniques listed for estimating a max HR. The secret to achieving a more exact number is to check max HR again (using the same testing technique you chose earlier) after you've been following your plan and workouts for a while. Do focus your training on using the best max HR number you have to date, and accept that this is a good number for now. Max HR is a journey for most of us, so be confident that the technique for estimating your personal max HR will point you on the right road to improving your fitness.

Different Sports, Different Max HRs

Your heart does have one true max HR, and it's genetically determined (you're born with it). The running max HR is the best approximation of your genetically determined max HR. That's because there are more large muscle groups involved in running than in swimming or biking. Max HR in the swim or on the bike could also be different from the run due to your different skill levels in each sport. Here are suggestions for how to test your swim max HR and bike max HR.

Swim Max HR Test

Swimming is likely to produce a lower sport-specific max HR because of your body position (horizontal) and the water supporting your body weight. Upper-body sports activities such as swimming tend to test around ten beats lower than running does even for very fit people.

To be safe, tell the lifeguard at the pool that you are doing a strenuous swim set and/or have a friend come along to help. A max HR test in the pool might look like this: Warm up. Swim several good hard lengths of the pool, then take a one-minute rest. Do two lengths of the pool as hard as you can without stopping. Repeat the two-length effort as many as six times, and check your HR between repeats. At some point, you will see your highest number for the session, and most likely the next few repeats will produce lower heart rates as you start to fatigue. The highest number you see on your monitor is your swim max HR. Be sure to cool down after this test and count it as a hard swim workout!

Bike Max HR Test

There is some disagreement among expert bikers and elite runners as to whether your max HR for the bike is likely to be lower than your running max HR. You may see very similar HR numbers for your cycling and running. All that matters is that you write down the number you see and retest at regular intervals.

Triathlete Lisa Oei trains with a Polar heart rate monitor.

Biking max HR can be determined by either placing your bike on a stationary stand or using a stationary bike. This keeps the road and weather conditions from being a distraction while you hammer on the pedals, and allows you to focus on your test rather than watching for traffic. Attach the watch part of the heart rate monitor to the handlebars so you can see it easily.

Warm up with increasing resistance by shifting up gears or increasing pedal speed (cadence) for five minutes. When you are fast and only just comfortable, hammer on those pedals for sixty seconds as fast as you can, then take a thirty-second rest. Repeat through five sprints of this kind. The highest number you see will be your bike max HR—probably in the fourth or fifth sprint. Be sure to cool down with an easy and slow cadence and little to no resistance.

Rebecca Yao, left, with Sally, center, at a Danskin Triathlon retailer seminar. Go to www.Danskin.com to find a list of free triathlon seminars.

Training with Your HRM in the Zones

My book *The Heart Rate Monitor Guidebook to Heart Zone Training* gives additional information about developing and keeping a healthy heart, managing your weight, and getting creative with your fitness program. Fit and unfit people burn fat differently. Training in different heart zones is one of the best ways to burn the maximum amount of fat in the least amount of time. For example, the more fit you are, the more effectively you use fat as a source of calories when you exercise. That's because the more fit you are, the more total calories you can burn at a given heart rate. Fit people are fat-burning machines. Because oxygen must be present for fat to burn in the muscles during exercise, unfit people need to exercise in very low heart zones to maximize fat burning. The best way to manage this is to apply heart rate technology.

Triathletes also want to increase their fitness, become more lean, and find ways to keep motivated in their training program but in a multisport context. However, if you are looking to start exercising with the training goal of finishing a triathlon, you'll want to familiarize yourself with *The Heart Rate Monitor Guidebook*. It's great background reading for this section and should be consulted if your triathlon goals include the challenges of weight management and increasing your activity level.

HEART ZONE TRAINING®

MAXIMUM HEART RATE

Training Zone [% maximum heart rate]	Fuel Burning	Max HR 150	Max HR 155	Max HR 160	Max HR 165	Max HR 170	Max HR 175	Max HR 180	Max HR 185	Max HR 190	Max HR 195	Max HR 200	Max HR 205	Max HR 210	Max HR 215	Max HR 220
Z5 RED LINE 90%-100%	GLYCOGEN BURNING	150	155	160	165	170	175	180	185	190	195	200	205	210	215	220
		135	140	144	149	153	158	162	167	171	176	180	185	189	194	198
Z4 THRESHOLD 80%-90%		135	140	144	149	153	158	162	167	171	176	180	185	189	194	198
		120	124	128	132	136	140	144	148	152	156	160	164	168	172	176
Z3 AEROBIC 70%-80%		120	124	128	132	136	140	144	148	152	156	160	164	168	172	176
		105	109	112	116	119	123	126	130	133	137	140	144	147	151	154
Z2 TEMPERATE 60%-70%	FAT BURNING	105	109	112	116	119	123	126	130	133	137	140	144	147	151	154
		90	93	96	99	102	105	108	111	114	117	120	123	126	129	132
Z1 HEALTHY HEART 50%-60%		90	93	96	99	102	105	108	111	114	117	120	123	126	129	132
		75	78	80	83	85	88	90	93	95	98	100	103	105	108	110

5 STEPS TO BETTER FITNESS AND PERFORMANCE

1. Choose your Heart Zone: Select one of the five different training zones based on the exercise goals for your workout.
2. Set your Maximum Heart Rate: Find your maximum heart rate (Max HR) along the top horizontal row of numbers.
3. Determine your Training Zone: The box where your selected training zone and Max HR column intersect is your heart rate training zone.
4. Set the Zone: The lower heart rate number in this box is the floor of your training zone and the upper number is the ceiling.
5. Stay in Zone: During each workout, maintain your heart rate between your zone floor and ceiling (excluding warm up and cool down).

© Copyright 1997 by Heart Zones Company, 2636 Fulton Avenue, Suite 200, Sacramento, CA 95821
Voice: (916) 481-7283. Fax: (916) 481-2213. Email: Sally.EDBBA.net. Website: www.heartzone.com

The Five Heart Zones

Heart zones are expressed as a percentage of your max HR. They reflect exercise intensity. By training in each of the five different zones, you'll realize five different results. Using your heart rate, you'll set each of these zones at 10 percent increments of your max HR. The heart zones training chart on page 13 shows you how.

Along the top of the chart, select the number that corresponds best to your max HR. You may want to concentrate on one or two zones per week while you are adapting your previous workout schedule to the concepts of heart zones training. This is a goal-based workout system based on using information from your monitor to better manage your fitness plan. Eventually, you'll train on different days in one or more of the five different heart zones using the max HR you've established in the three sports. This is called "time in zone" training, and here's what happens in each of them:

- ## Zone 1, The Healthy Heart Zone:
  50%–60% of your individual max HR (RPE 1–2)

  This is the safest, most comfortable zone, reached by walking briskly, swimming easily, or doing any low-intensity activity including mowing your lawn. Here you strengthen your heart and improve muscle mass while you reduce body fat, cholesterol, blood pressure, and your risk for degenerative disease. You get healthier in this zone but not more aerobically fit—that is, it won't increase your endurance or strength, but it will improve your health.

- ## Zone 2, The Temperate Zone:
  60%–70% of your individual max HR (RPE 3–4)

  Zone 2 is easily reached by going a little faster, such as increasing from a walk to a jog. Although still a relatively low level of effort, this zone starts training your body to increase the rate of fat released from the cells to the muscles for fuel. Some people have erroneously called this the "fat-burning zone" because up to 85 percent of the total calories burned in this zone are fat calories, but in truth we burn fat in all zones.

- ## Zone 3, The Aerobic Zone:
  70%–80% of your individual max HR (RPE 5–6)

  In this zone—reached by running moderately, for example—you

improve your functional capacity. The number and size of your blood vessels increase, your lung capacity and respiratory rate improve, and your heart increases in size and strength. The result is that you can exercise longer before becoming fatigued. You're still metabolizing fats and carbohydrates, but the ratio has changed to about 50-50, which means both are burning at the same rate.

• Zone 4, The Threshold Zone:
80%–90% of your individual max HR (RPE 7–8)

This zone is reached by going hard—running faster. Here you get faster and fitter, increasing your heart rate as you cross from aerobic to anaerobic training. At this point, your heart cannot pump enough blood and oxygen to supply the exercising muscles fully, so they respond by continuing to contract anaerobically (without sufficient oxygen). This is where you "feel the burn." You can stay in this zone for a limited amount of time, usually not more than an hour. That's because the muscle just cannot sustain working anaerobically without fatiguing.

New Rating of Perceived Exertion (RPE)

There's a chart called the rating of perceived exertion (RPE) that shows you how to correlate how you feel—your perceived exertion—to your heart rate. It is not a precise measurement, but perceived exertion is another way to quantify exercise intensity.

The problem is just this—perceived exertion using only your personal perceptions of effort to set your training intensities misses the target. It was quantified by exercise scientist Dr. Gunnar Borg in 1973 when he first based a rating scale on perceived exertion.

Foster's American Version Rating of Perceived Exertion

Rate of Perceived Exertion (RPE)	Feeling
0	Rest
1	Very, very easy
2	Easy
3	Moderate
4	Somewhat hard
5	Hard
6	Hard!
7	Very hard!
8	Very, very hard!
9	Extremely hard!
10	Maximal

Some researchers have found that perceived exertion can be very accurate. Others report it to be unacceptably inaccurate. It's my opinion that if you want to train with clear and accurate information, using the guess method attached to your feelings is probably not the soundest way.

The working muscles protect themselves from overwork by not being able to maintain the intensity level.

- ### Zone 5, The Red-Line Zone:
  #### 90%–100% of your individual max HR (RPE 9–10)

  This is the equivalent of running all-out and is used mostly as an "interval" training regimen—exertion done only in short- to intermediate-length bursts. Even world-class athletes can stay in this zone for only a few minutes at a time. It's not a zone most people will select for exercise, since working out here hurts and there is an increased potential for injury. You do burn lots of calories, mostly carbohydrates.

The Training Wheel

Now you understand that we use the beat of our heart as the source of determining how hard we exercise. Most people have been using how

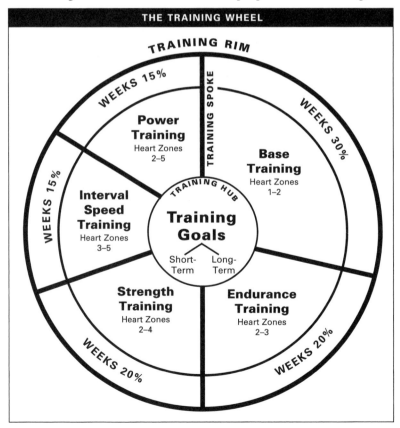

	SELF-TEST SCORE CARD		
Fitness Categories	**1.5-Mile Run** Time Score	**400-Yard Swim** Time Score	**3-Mile Bike Ride** Time Score
High		5:01 20.0	5:53 20.0
		5:07 19.5	6:00 19.5
		5:13 19.0	6:08 19.0
		5:20 18.5	6:17 18.5
	8:05 18.0	5:27 18.0	6:26 18.0
	8:20 17.5	5:34 17.5	6:35 17.5
	8:35 17.0	5:41 17.0	6:45 17.0
	8:55 16.5	5:49 16.5	6:55 16.5
	9:10 16.0	5:57 16.0	7:05 16.0
	9:31 15.5	6:05 15.5	7:17 15.5
	9:50 15.0	6:14 15.0	7:29 15.0
	10:16 14.5	6:23 14.5	7:41 14.5
Medium	10:35 14.0	6:32 14.0	7:54 14.0
	11:01 13.5	6:42 13.5	8:08 13.5
	11:31 13.0	6:53 13.0	8:23 13.0
	12:01 12.5	7:04 12.5	8:39 12.5
	12:35 12.0	7:16 12.0	8:56 12.0
	13:10 11.5	7:28 11.5	9:14 11.5
	13:50 11.0	7:41 11.0	9:33 11.0
	14:31 10.5	7:55 10.5	9:54 10.5
	15:20 10.0	8:10 10.0	10:16 10.0
	16:10 9.5	8:26 9.5	10:40 9.5
Low	17:16 9.0	8:43 9.0	11:05 9.0
	18:25 8.5	9:01 8.5	11:33 8.5
	19:40 8.0	9:20 8.0	12:04 8.0
	21:16 7.5	9:41 7.5	12:37 7.5
		10:03 7.0	13:13 7.0
		10:27 6.5	13:53 6.5
		10:53 6.0	14:37 6.0
		11:21 5.5	15:26 5.5
		11:52 5.0	16:21 5.0
		12:25 4.5	
		13:02 4.0	

they feel, or they might use how fast they ride or run. With the technology of a heart rate monitor, you don't have to guess any longer; rather, you can train precisely. To do this we use the analogy of riding around the training wheel. There's more information on this training wheel in Chapter 6.

You go around the wheel of your training wheel at your own speed. As you do so you'll increase your all-around fitness, and your body will experience wonderful, truly incredible changes. The different training spokes on the training wheel, like the different heart zones, are based on the benefits you receive when you are training in them. Clockwise from the top, the spokes are as follows: base spoke, endurance spoke, strength spoke, interval speed spoke, power spoke.

Self-Tests to Determine Your Starting Spoke on the Training Wheel

Where to start on your training wheel depends on your current level of fitness. The only way to know if you are getting fitter and accomplishing your goals is to set some benchmarks to evaluate your present physical condition. To start, make sure you are at a comfortable base level of training. To test yourself at each sport, do a 1.5-mile run, a 400-yard swim, and a 3-mile bike ride, making an all-out speed effort at each. Take the tests on different days to allow adequate rest between each so that you can perform at your best. Then, using the self-test scorecard, determine whether you fall into a high-, medium-, or low-fitness category, according to your performance in each activity. Repeat these tests on a regular basis to measure improved performance.

A wave start at a Danskin Triathlon.

THREE

BASIC MOVES FOR SWIMMING

Swim Biomechanics

For practical reasons, the most efficient stroke used in triathlons is the freestyle (also known as the "crawl"). The breaststroke, the backstroke, the butterfly, and others simply are not as efficient or as quick as the freestyle.

Think of the body as a lever system—the bones are straight lines, like rigid sticks, and the joints are hinges, like the hinges that swing doors open and closed. Pictured this way, the body is a stick figure with the joints as places around which the sticks rotate.

In the biomechanics of swimming, your job is simple—move your sticks around their hinges by contracting the right muscles at the right time. This is obviously extremely simplified. Kinesiologists would love to turn this discussion into one about torques, levers, angles of pull and resistance, pulleys, and equations dealing with power. For our uses, though, the sticks-and hinges-model will work fine.

When you swim and are thinking in terms of putting together the various movements of your stroke, visualize this stick figure and break down the freestyle into the individual movement of each stick part.

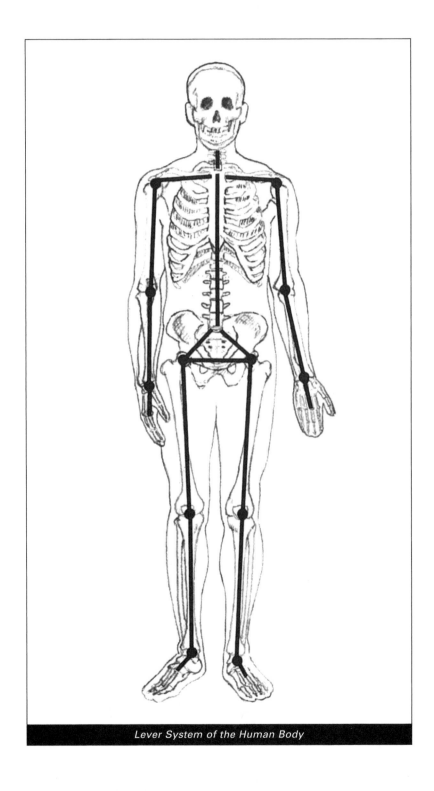

Lever System of the Human Body

The Big Stick: Body Position

The more streamlined your sticks are, the less resistance they will cause and the faster you will move. Compared with a fish, we aren't very streamlined, but we compensate a great deal with the positioning of our limbs to reduce our body's drag against the water.

It used to be that swimmers would try to lie as flat as possible, with the body parallel to the surface of the water. The assumption was that this was the most hydrodynamic position. The new thinking for swimming is to spend more time at an angle on your side, with your hand extended above your head and your head positioned so that you're looking straight down at the bottom of the pool. This makes you longer, with a silhouette more like a fish; therefore you have less resistance and can go faster for less energy expense. Rather than pushing the water with your shoulders, you're slicing through it with your hand extended to your full reach. Don't hang your head, and don't look forward except to see the pool wall. Keep your spine straight, from your head down to your hips—don't swivel at the waist. Core strength, meaning the strength of your chest, abs, and back, is very important to swimming. Use that core to power your arms and keep your legs up.

Kicking is not a major part of distance swimming (i.e., distances over 200 yards such as the 500 or 1,000). Generally, aim for a two-beat kick (each leg kicks once with each arm rotation) when you're swimming, simply to keep your legs up. You don't want your legs to drag down, which would increase your resistance in the water. But you also don't want to expend a lot of energy in your kick, especially with a bike ride and a run ahead of you. You will also use the strength of your abs and back to keep your legs up, by pressing down with your chest and head.

As you breathe through your mouth, roll partway to the side and twist your neck hinge on its axis, just enough to get air, without lifting your head.

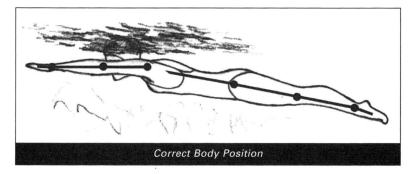

Correct Body Position

Your head creates a trough or hole in the water called a "bow wave." After you rotate your head, breathe in with your mouth inside the bow wave.

Just as cars go out of alignment and need to be realigned, so do swimmers. The three common body alignment mistakes and diagnoses are as follows:

MISTAKE 1: The body is not level enough in the water.
Solution: Failure to maintain a level position is usually caused by trying to lift the head too high, with a resulting drop of the lower body, or by not kicking efficiently, which results in the dropping of the lower body.

MISTAKE 2: The body moves sideways (laterally).
Solution: Lateral movement can be caused by moving the head out of alignment, which tends to force the body sideways; also, lateral movement of the arms, rather than vertical movement of the arms, tends to produce lateral movement of the body.

MISTAKE 3: The body doesn't roll enough.
Solution: Roll is necessary—your torso and legs should roll from side to side to such an extent that your shoulders will alternately point toward the pool bottom.

The problem with arranging all of your sticks (bones) into the correct alignment is that it is very difficult to visualize yourself as you swim. Ask someone knowledgeable, such as a coach or fellow swimmer, to check your body positioning in the water regularly. Programs such as the Danskin Mentor-Mentee program, which matches up first-timers with experienced triathletes, can offer opportunities to learn a lot from people who have experience in each individual sport (visit www.mentormentee.org for more information). Masters swim programs also offer you a good way to get more time in the water with a coach and other swimmers.

The Arm and Hand Stick: The S-Shaped Curve

You will know it because you will feel it—most swimming power comes from the arm and shoulder muscles. If we could focus on only one aspect of swimming, it would have to be the action of the arm stick.

The arm is made up of the following sticks and hinges: the shoulder joint, the upper arm, the elbow joint, the lower arm, the wrist joint, and the hand. Each of these must be coordinated to maximize propulsion.

When your hand first breaks water, thumb first, it moves forward to full extension. In sequence, the wrist turns; the hand presses out and downward, then scoops inward; the elbow stays high and bends as the hand draws an S-shaped curve as it moves under the body. Then, with the elbow at a right angle, the hand pushes straight backward and your pulling arm accelerates quickly. Near the end of the pull phase, your elbow extends from the 90-degree position. You are now at the center of the S curve that your hand is drawing.

Push your hand back, not out or up, until your elbow is fully extended. As the thumb passes parallel to the thigh, it starts upward and breaks the water's surface with the smallest fingers first. Simultaneously, the opposite hand breaks the water's surface in front of your face and begins the S curve.

THE S-SHAPED CURVE

Pointers

• During the first part of the stroke, the elbow should be higher than the hand.

• The hand should stay below the body in the water, not out to the side.

• When the arm is extended forward, there should be a brief pause while the other arm strokes. This makes you longer in the water, which helps you move faster. The goal is to move farther with fewer strokes.

• During arm recovery (the time the arm is out of the water) the elbow initially leads the way, and your hand should pass the elbow only when the hand has reached the shoulder point.

• As you pull, imagine reaching over a barrel— that's how it should feel. Press down with your shoulder, using your body strength, to add power to the stroke.

The Leg Stick: The Two-Beat Flutter Kick

The primary purposes of the legs during the flutter kick are stability first and forward motion second, since the legs offer very little propulsive force while you are swimming long distances. The stick-and-hinge sequence is as follows: the hip joint, the upper leg, the knee joint, the lower leg, the ankle joint, the foot.

The leg-stick action consists of two upbeats and two downbeats per arm cycle. Since these two directions—up and down—are perpendicular to your direction of travel, it may seem almost counterproductive to kick. It's not. The flutter kick is a very important aspect of the crawl.

It is vital to note that the up-and-down leg movement must not be rigid, or it will cancel itself out. This is one reason swimmers are flexible—they must have a large range of motion, particularly of the feet and ankles, to allow for forward propulsion, because the feet serve as flippers.

The legs contribute to streamlining and body positioning (alignment) and especially help keep the body from falling prey to the problem of lateral weaving. To be stable, you must flex your hip and push downward with your thigh as you begin the downbeat, and point your toes upward and backward. Because the body rolls as you kick, there is a slight kick outward, as well. Your downbeat is finished when the leg is completely straight and just below your body.

Estelle Gray learning to love swimming.

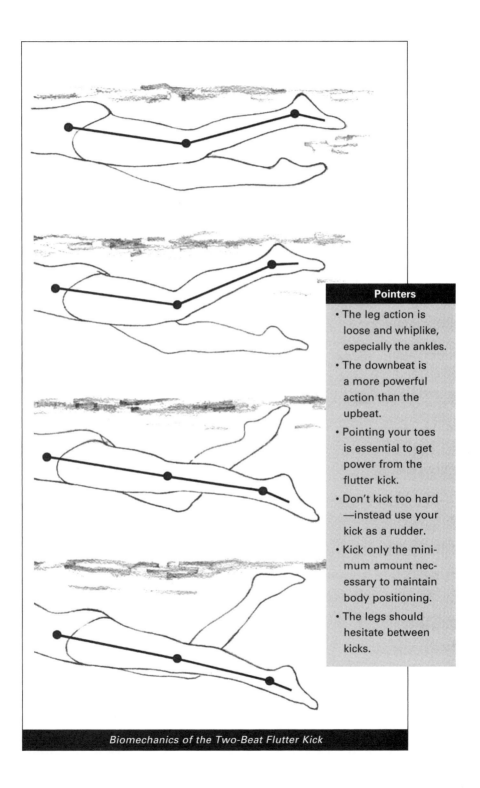

Pointers

- The leg action is loose and whiplike, especially the ankles.
- The downbeat is a more powerful action than the upbeat.
- Pointing your toes is essential to get power from the flutter kick.
- Don't kick too hard —instead use your kick as a rudder.
- Kick only the minimum amount necessary to maintain body positioning.
- The legs should hesitate between kicks.

Biomechanics of the Two-Beat Flutter Kick

The upbeat is a rebound-like action. When the leg is fully extended, you sweep it up, passing the downbeat of the opposite leg. One of the most common mistakes new swimmers make is bending their knees during the upbeat. Keep your knee extended, and it will prevent drag. With the upbeat, as the leg goes toward the surface, use the hip flexors with a relaxed lower leg and ankle.

Swim Training

Swimming uses a different training system, one based on high volume and intensity, from either cycling or running. Competitive swimming events tend to be short, as opposed to most cycling or running races. Thus most of a swimmer's training time is spent practicing the events that will be raced and working on technique, rather than simply swimming long distances.

Swimmers follow the interval training system, a method of using multiple, timed, repeat swims in a combination of rest and intensity. An example of the interval training system is to swim five 100-yard swim repeats at 80 percent effort, with 30 seconds of rest between each repeat swim.

An acronym for this format of swim intervals, and a way to help trigger your memory of the four parts to a set, is "RIND," which stands for *rest, intensity, number,* and *distance.* A rind such as that of an orange or apple is the shell that encases something; in this case, RIND is the shell that encases the interval training system. All sets contain a RIND:

R = the rest interval between each repeat (in our example, R = 30 seconds)

I = the intensity of each repeat (in this example, I = 80 percent)
    Some swim coaches like to express intensity in other
    terms such as
    • A specific heart rate like 150–160 beats/minute, or 75 percent
      of your max HR
    • A specific departure time from the wall, such as at every 1 minute
    • A perceived exertion rate, such as 7 on a scale of 10

N = the number of repeats in the set (in above example, N = five repeats)

D = the distance of each of the repeats (in our example, D = 100 yards)

Keep in mind that although most pools still are measured in yards, some are measured in meters, and since triathlon race distances are generally in metric terms, you'll need to be prepared to make the distance conversions.

For that purpose, 1 yard = 0.91 meters, and 1 meter = 1.09 yards. For example, the Danskin Women's Triathlon Series has a swim segment of 750 meters, or 817.5 yards.

When you design your swim workout, you will be varying your RIND, the four parts to the interval training system. Here are some suggestions for how to build and vary your swim workouts:

(R) *Rest interval between each repeat:* Rest intervals are usually described as a ratio between the amount of time spent swimming and the amount of time spent resting. Hence, a 5:1 ratio means five minutes of swimming and one minute of resting. The rule of thumb is to keep the rest interval less than one-half the time of the swim, or no more than a 2:1 ratio. The most common ratios are 3:1 or 4:1. This means that if you swim a repeat of 50 yards in 45 seconds, a 3:1 ratio will entail a 15-second rest. Typically, the short rest periods improve aerobic fitness more effectively than the longer ones. Here are some suggested rest intervals based upon the distance of the repeat:

OPTIMUM REST INTERVALS FOR REPEAT SWIM DISTANCES	
Distance	Rest Interval
25 yards/meters	5–10 seconds
50 yards/meters	10–20 seconds
75–100 yards/meters	10–45 seconds
150–200 yards/meters	20–60 seconds
200–400 yards/meters	45 seconds–2 minutes
400 yards/meters and longer	1–3 minutes

(I) *Intensity of each interval:* The best method of maintaining an accurate amount of intensity is by using heart rate as your measuring scale. Since taking your pulse after each interval simply isn't practical, I urge you to use one of the commercial heart rate monitors for swimmers that are available. Most swimmers, though, rely on their subjective perceptions of how hard they are swimming and periodically manually check their heart rate.

(N) *Number of repeats:* A group of interval repeats is called a set. Each set should last no less and not much more than ten minutes in total swim and rest time. Ten minutes is the minimum amount of time for a set, because it takes about three to four minutes for your body to warm up to training

Kathy Nishizahi, left, one of the first members of Team Survivor–San Jose, died of breast cancer in 2000. She is pictured with her coach, Lisa Talbott.

intensity. The balance of the time is then devoted to stressing the body's cardiorespiratory system so that the training effect can occur. The training effect is the improvement to the entire physiological system that occurs as a result of exercise, which enhances your overall athletic performance, no matter the sport.

(**D**) *Distance of each repeat:* The training effect is not as dependent on the distance of each repeat as it is on the length of time of the entire set. So, to offset boredom, vary your repeats using distances from 25 meters up to several hundred. In a short-course pool, that is, one that is 25 meters in length, a 50-meter repeat will obviously require you to swim continuously for two lengths, whereas in a long-course (50-meter) pool, a 50-meter repeat will only require you to swim one length.

If you can join a swim group, do so. They are motivating, social, and may have a coach who can provide you with biomechanical advice. Using rest intervals usually doesn't work with groups, however, because there are generally multiple swimmers in a lane, and some are ready to start while others are resting. Therefore, in this situation swimmers use "departure time" rather than rest intervals.

A departure time is the sum of the rest interval and swim interval times. In our example, the departure time equals the rest interval, 30 seconds, plus the length of time it takes you to swim 50 yards—let's say 45 seconds. So, you would add 30 seconds and 45 seconds, and your departure time would equal 1 minute and 15 seconds. You would then depart from the wall for each repeat at the 1 minute and 15 second (1:15) point, as indicated by the pace clock. Some coaches would write this set as follows: 5 x 50 yards @ 1:15.

As your conditioning improves, your departure times will drop. After several weeks it may surprise you, because for the same perceived effort, you will be able to use a 1 minute and 10 second departure time and feel that the workload is the same. This is the training effect—you'll become stronger and fitter faster.

Workouts

Any swim workout, regardless of your skill level, should consist of a warm-up period, the main set, and a cooldown period.

Sample workout for a beginning swimmer:

Warm up: Swim 100 yards (4 lengths of a 25-yard pool) to warm up. Swim continuously if you can; if you can't, rest at the end of each length until you're ready to go again.

Main set: Swim 4 x 25 yards, with 15–30 seconds rest after each. Use each repeat to work on your stroke mechanics (swim drills).

Cool down: Swim 50 yards at a slow pace to cool down.

This workout is only 250 yards, or 10 lengths of the pool, but it's a great start. As you improve, you can increase the number of repeats or the distances, or both, to increase the distance you're capable of completing. You want to work up to swimming at least 750 meters continuously, since that's what you'll be doing in a sprint triathlon. Remember, it's not important to swim as fast as you can; rather you need to be able to swim continuously for 750 meters. You don't want to try to race this, since you'll have to bike and run afterward.

Sample workout for an intermediate swimmer:
Warm up: Swim for 250 yards.

Main set: 1. Swim 6 x 50 yards, with 15 seconds rest between each.

2. Kick or pull for 200 yards, depending on whether you want to work your arms or legs (optional).

3. Swim 2 x 100 yards with 20–30 seconds rest between each.

Cool down: Swim for 50–100 yards.

This intermediate-level workout will give you a total swim length of 1,000–1,050 yards.

You can change the parts of a workout however you prefer, going shorter or longer distances or doing more repeats. Tailor the workouts to your ability and comfort, and vary what you do or the intensity. Doing the same thing repeatedly can cause boredom or even lead to injury. Remember, use RIND to work on different aspects of swim training: rest time, intensity, number of repeats, and distance.

One way to work on your stroke mechanics is to use drills. This trains your muscle memory to do things correctly, giving you more efficiency in the water. For example, many new swimmers lift their hands out of the water first, rather than their elbows. To correct this, during a workout spend a couple of lengths dragging your fingertips across the surface of the water during the upstroke (when your arm is out of the water). This will force you to raise your elbow, which should always be above your hand as you stroke. When your arm breaks out of the water at the end of a stroke, your elbow should come first and stay high. Your hand should not pass the elbow until it's past your ear.

Another drill is to do one full revolution of each arm while your other arm stays out in front of you. As you stroke with your right arm, roll onto your left side, holding your left arm extended straight ahead of you (pointing toward the end of the pool, not the bottom). As your right arm comes up past your head on the upstroke, begin to roll toward your right side. When your right hand reaches your left hand, begin to stroke with the left hand while you roll over toward the right. Remember to keep your body and spine straight, with no twisting, and hold your right arm straight. This will help you learn proper rolling technique and help you stretch out and go farther with each stroke. Always do drills at a slow pace, and keep yourself focused on your form instead of your speed. Drills are also good to do as a cooldown.

In training for a triathlon, it's a good idea to swim the distance of the race at least once during your training, several weeks to a month before the race. If you are a reasonably strong swimmer, you might want to over-distance train, or swim farther than the race distance, which will prepare you for race day. Since most pools are measured in yards and the race is measured in meters, you need to know how far to go. Use the multiplier of 1.09 yards for each meter; here's how it works:

750 meters x 1.09 = 817.5 yards
For an over-distance swim, I recommend going 1,000 yards (910 meters).

You can also use a steady-state heart rate test to see how you've improved. Time yourself swimming a set distance, such as 500 or 1000 yards, keeping your heart rate steady in your aerobic zone (70–80 percent of your max HR). Every month or so of training, repeat the test. With training, you should take less and less time to swim the same distance at the same heart rate. This is a great way to gauge your progress in the water.

Open-Water Swims

It is a good idea to practice swimming in open water before the race. On race day, you'll be starting in the water with a wave of other women, up to about 100 people. (At the Ironman in Hawaii, all 1,500-plus people start together!) If you train with a group, plan to get together and practice this start. At some races, people will be in such a hurry to get going that they can swim right over you or accidentally kick or hit you while they're swimming. I recommend that people who aren't strong swimmers start toward the back or off to the side to avoid this risk.

Many people are afraid of the open water, since unlike in a pool, the bottom is usually invisible, and there are no walls in case you get tired. If the swim is in a lake or pond, there is also generally some type of vegetation, or, if the swim is in the ocean, there are waves. There will be lifeguards on paddleboards and in boats during the race to help you if you need it. If you can, try to swim the actual racecourse as part of your training; it can make a tremendous difference to your confidence level, since you'll know on race day that you can do it.

However, never swim in open water by yourself. Take along a training partner, swim with a group, or have a friend in a canoe or kayak to help you if you get tired. Swimming through duckweed and waves is a very different experience from doing laps in a pool, and for your own safety you need to have someone on hand to help you out of difficulties.

Open-water swims are also the perfect time to work on your sighting. During the triathlon, swimmers need to lift their heads every few strokes to make sure they're heading in the right direction. You simply bring your head up out of the water and look ahead for the buoy or the finish, while you continue to stroke with your arms. Practice this regularly, so it's a comfortable part of your stroke. Without sighting, you can end up swimming from one side of the course to the other, especially if it's a wide swim course, and thus swim a lot farther than you need to.

Waiting at the starting line for their wave,
two women triathletes plan their swim route.

BASIC MOVES FOR BICYCLING

Bike Biomechanics

In the bike world, the buzzwords are "handling skills," the biomechanical riding techniques that involve your ability to control a bike effectively and efficiently. Before you can begin to practice handling skills, though, you must have a bike frame that fits your body frame. If you don't match frames, you will never achieve effective bike-handling skills. Also, your bike rides longer than ten miles will be plagued with sore shoulders, wrists, knees, and ankles, not to mention posteriors!

You can spend a lot of money and buy the best possible bike, with a great paint job and the finest components, but if it doesn't fit you, you are likely to be miserable. No, it's more than likely—you *will* be miserable.

Buying a Bike That Fits

Don't take the usual advice "Just go to the shop, and they can look at you and tell you what size bike to buy." All you know about that salesperson sizing you up is that he or she gets paid to do it; you don't know if the person has any expertise.

Take this advice instead—go to a specialty bike shop and get measured. (If you don't know of a shop, get a recommendation from a woman bicyclist cruising by on your local bike trail.) About once a year the major cycling magazines publish articles on sizing and bike fit, which are also often available at their websites. Commercial sizing systems such as the Fit Kit, BioRacer, and Serotta's Size-Cycle can be very helpful. The Fit Kit is available in most quality bike and triathlon stores. A store might apply the Fit Kit cost against the purchase price of the bike if you ask in advance. The analysis takes about thirty minutes, and you will be given a complete written set of measurements of what fits your individual anatomy: saddle height, frame size, crank length, handlebar stem length, and much more.

Next, test ride several different bikes that are the right frame size.

Anatomical Differences and Bike Fit

Obviously, anatomical differences affect how bikes fit the human frame. If bikes were fit by height alone, there would be no need for different frame sizes. But bikes are divided into two separately measured units by the seat, which must be fitted to two different parts of the human body: the upper body (torso) and the lower body (leg). The two measurements—torso and leg length—are very different between women and men, and these differences necessitate modifications in bike design.

Bicycle fit involves compromises. You must compromise between comfort on the one hand, and performance, quick acceleration and handling stability, and top speed on the other. You may notice that some bikes aren't completely comfortable for you. That is because most bikes are designed for men's anatomies, not for the size and shape of women's bodies. Today, you can find bikes designed for women like the Stellar Rodriguez from R&E Cycles (Seattle, Washington).

I race on an R&E's Rodriquez beam bike that Estelle Gray and her business partner Dan Towle helped to design with their frame builder,

---

Shifter Systems

Although you could shop for a good bike-frame fit and a comfortable seat, you might want to start by considering shifters. What type of shifters you like could determine what bike (road, mountain, cross, or tri) you ultimately like. In biking, you are always shifting, and smooth gear shifting makes a big difference in how much you enjoy your bike. Some systems are grip shifters, on the ends of the handlebars, and these require using your wrist. Some are finger shifters. Campagnolo shifters involve a push with the fingers and thumbs. Shimano requires a little larger hand than average because you have to push the brake lever. So consider wrists and fingers, because you are always shifting!

Matt Houle. It's faster than the winds can gust! My bike is specifically built for my measurements and comes from a shop with a long history of top-quality handcrafted bikes for women. I couldn't ask for better equipment. And at the 1998 Ironman in Hawaii, I still had a bike ride that challenged my bike skills.

During that ride, the twentieth anniversary of the Hawaiian Ironman Triathlon, at mile 25 on the 110-mile bike course, I was pedaling at 85 percent of my maximum heart rate, on a steep downhill, in my smallest chainring (the one I use to climb steep uphills, not to handle downhills), and my bike computer read an excruciatingly slow 8 mph. At the bottom of the hill, I began climbing up the other side and saw it read 4–6 mph, and I didn't have any lower gears to shift down to (nor did anyone else). Throughout most of that section of the bike race (about 40 miles), all of us had to lean into the wind, at a near 45-degree tilt so that the gusts wouldn't blow us over. In fact, several athletes were actually knocked off their bikes because of the impact of the winds, and on several occasions I was hit and blown across the centerline on the highway. That's the nature of the Ironman course in Hawaii. I named the new bike Heartbeat, and it performed like a champion through those fierce South Pacific winds, the heat, and my spilling fluid electrolyte drink all over it!

Sally Edwards in the 1998 Hawaiian Ironman riding a Rodriguez custom bicycle with a Softride beam named "Heartbeat."

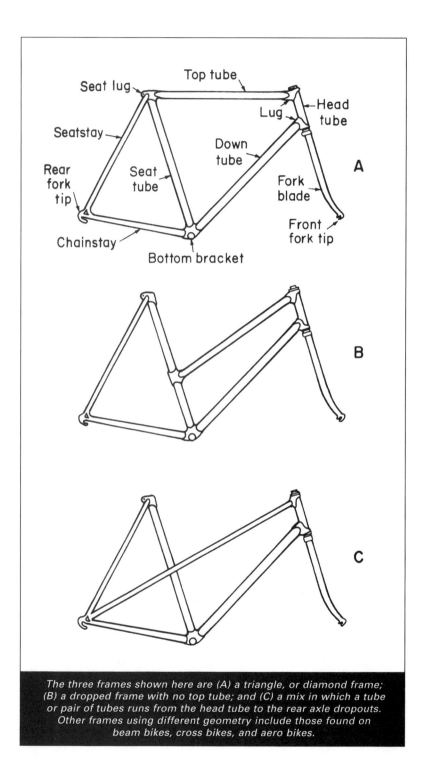

The three frames shown here are (A) a triangle, or diamond frame; (B) a dropped frame with no top tube; and (C) a mix in which a tube or pair of tubes runs from the head tube to the rear axle dropouts. Other frames using different geometry include those found on beam bikes, cross bikes, and aero bikes.

What Kind of Bike

When it comes time for your bicycle selection and fit, clamp down hard on the brakes and give the matter careful consideration. There is much to know, and the information can be conflicting. Basically, there are two parts to bicycles: the frame and the components. When you purchase a stock bike, you take these together and work with your shop to swap out—for additional dollars—what parts you'd like to upgrade. Bicycles are relatively simple machines that can be reduced to wheels, seat, frame, wires, chain, and gears with a couple of wrenches and screwdrivers. There are road bikes, mountain bikes, triathlon bikes, and cross bikes. Decide what role the bicycle plays in your life, and then buy the best one that fits your body and suits your purpose.

Now that you know some of the basics of bike fit, here are the biomechanics of riding and handling your bike.

Cycling Techniques

Once you've become acquainted with (your second self) your bike, it's time to introduce the handling skills that will get you where you want to go.

If it's your first lesson, it's a good idea to find a quiet street or parking lot to practice. The first biking technique to master is the foot-to-the-pedal action. If you have toe clips, turn the crank so that the free pedal is in the 1 o'clock position. Tap the back edge of the pedal with your toe, turning the pedal to the upright position, and slide your foot into the cage. The position is awkward at first, but once you are in and have tightened the toe strap, you will be snugly joined to your bike. You will eventually do the same with your other pedal, but for now leave one foot loose for emergency stops, until you gain confidence.

If you ride with clipless pedals, the process is a lot easier. Again, place the pedal perpendicular, in the lowest (6 o'clock) position, step into the clip with your heel high and toe pointed down, then push down firmly with your heel and listen for the "snick" as you snap yourself in. To release, rotate your foot and pedal to a position parallel to the ground and kick your heel out a bit, using the toe as a pivot point.

You're now ready to go. Don't be surprised, though, if you go down or crash at some point. A fall is an experience that happens to every rider. To minimize your chances of a crash, here are some tips on how to ride more efficiently and safely over a variety of conditions.

Riding the relay leg of Sacramento's Eppies Great Race, Mary Burroughs makes a tight turn using the proper riding technique.

Riding a Straight Line

This is the first technique you need to learn, and it's the one that might keep you from crashing during a race. Other cyclists assume that once you've started, you will continue to ride in a straight line without changing direction by even a few inches. That assumption is critical for you to appreciate, because if you are going to change direction, you must let the riders around you know.

Practice the technique of riding a straight line by actually riding on a line on a bike trail or parking lot. If you weave extensively, it could be because your bike doesn't fit you, because you have a bent frame or fork, or because you simply need more time in the saddle.

Cornering

To turn ("corner"), lean. Unless you are going extremely slowly, all your turns will be based on leaning into the turn, not turning the handlebars. Lean harder on the handlebar toward the turn and raise the *inside* pedal in a turn so you are grazing the top tube with the inside of your outside knee. If you are turning left, your *left* arm is pressing toward the left and your *left* knee is up and pressing *away from* the top tube. Survey your turn in advance, and pick a line (the path you will take) in the turn. Throughout the turn, hold your line.

Stopping

The dangers of using your front brakes to stop are mainly mythical—you won't go flying over your handlebars unless you hit your front brakes so hard that you nearly lock them. About 90 percent of your braking power comes from your front brakes, so use them. It's best to use both brakes in tandem, especially if you have to stop quickly. For slow stops, you can use your back brake alone if you wish. In the rain or on fast downhills, you should pump your brakes just as you would those of your car. Finally, for a slight reduction in speed, usually when you are riding closely behind another rider, "feather" your brakes by squeezing the brake levers slightly.

When you stop, always release your right foot from the pedal in advance. There is an obvious safety reason for releasing the right and not the left foot: If you do fall, you will fall to the right, away from the car lane. Slide off the saddle (seat) just as you come to a complete stop.

Spinning

This is a technique of pedaling rapidly (at a high number of revolutions per minute [rpm]) in low gears. The low gears are the easy ones to pedal; the high gears are difficult. Spinning allows you to work more efficiently by increasing your speed while decreasing the workload. It's like lifting weights —it's easier to lift a one-pound weight a hundred times than a fifty-pound weight twice.

For long-distance riding, most cyclists spin at a pedal cadence (the number of rotations or the rate that you spin) of 75–85 rpm, although there are some who prefer to spin at a cadence of up to 100-plus rpm.

If you don't have a cyclometer (also called a bike computer, a device that measures speed, cadence, and other important bicycling statistics),

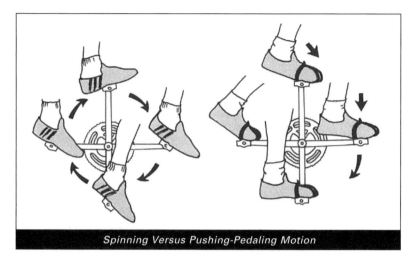

Spinning Versus Pushing-Pedaling Motion

you will have to count your pedal cadence. Count the number of rpm over a 10-second period and multiply by 6 to find your spin rate per minute. As you learn to spin, start by using extremely low gears and low resistance (ride on a flat course). If you train in low gears on the flats, you may be embarrassed at how slowly you travel, but you'll get the technique right.

Spinning is one of those techniques that a beginner needs as little as an hour to learn. However, if you already know how to ride, it may take you much longer, since breaking old habits, like braking a heavy vehicle, takes time. My book *The Heart Rate Monitor Book for Cyclists* takes an in-depth look at spin workouts and shows you more training tips for high-performance cycling.

Road Safety

Bicycles share the road with cars. When you bike, obey the road and traffic signals as you would in a car and travel in the same direction, staying to the right of the lane.

- Pedestrians have the right of way when you are on the bike. If there are parts of your route that necessitate your use of the sidewalk, please use it as a guest and re-enter the roadway as soon as you can.
- Never, never, never, ride with earphones, not even on a trail set aside for nonmotorized traffic. It's simply dumb.
- Dogs like things with wheels. Dogs like to chase things with wheels. Dogs don't like water squirted in their faces from water bottles. Now you know why you have two water bottle cages.

- Why be a purist? Drive to the good spots for biking and avoid riding through the traffic. If you want to practice a favorite hill, try it before the daily commute gets going.
- When you pass another rider, it's a good practice to announce (shout), "Passing on your right (or left)." The rider you are passing probably doesn't know you are nearby but needs to know your position in order to ride safely.
- During group rides, if a car is coming from behind and you are at the back of the group, yell loudly to the front of the group "Car back," to let everyone know of the car's position. Likewise, if you are in the front and a car is approaching, yell "Car up."

Riding with a pack of cyclists requires fine-tuned handing skills. If you weave to miss a hole or dodge an object, you may veer into other cyclists and crash. When you attend your first group ride, hang back and learn, because when you are ready to ride in front, you will be responsible for letting the others know what is ahead. Some groups rely on hand signals for turns, potholes, slowing, stopping, and announcing an approaching car; other groups are more vocal.

Drafting

When you ride in packs, you "draft." Drafting is a technique of riding closely behind another cyclist in her slipstream. This allows the front rider to break the wind for you, so you can sit behind her and ride more easily. Riding the draft can save you about 15–20 percent of the energy requirements of riding solo.

Drafting, for that obvious reason, is not allowed in most triathlons. You will see drafting only in the Olympics and a few other events where the bike portion of a triathlon more closely resembles a bike race. However, at some point in your training you will probably ride with a group, so you'll need to know the skill. First, make sure that it's all right for you to draft— some riders don't want you "on their wheel." The way to ask is to say, "May I sit in?" If you don't ask, you can create a lot of anger.

As you ride in a draft position, you must be extremely focused, because you need intense concentration and skill to ride 6 inches to 2 feet behind the rear wheel of another cyclist. When there are several riders drafting, the line of riders is called an "echelon," or "paceline," and the rider in front

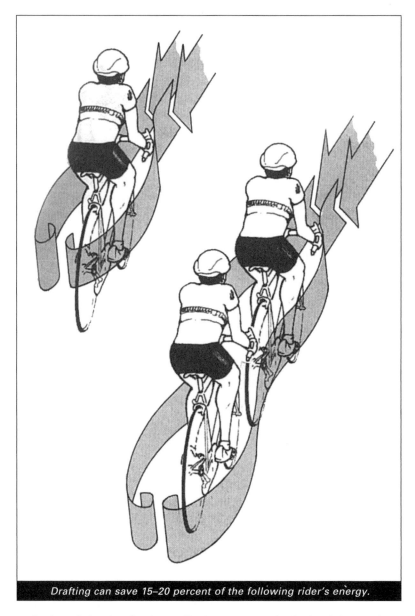

Drafting can save 15–20 percent of the following rider's energy.

pulls those behind. After her pull, she rotates to the back of the paceline, and the next rider in line takes the front position and pulls.

When it's your turn to pull, if you can't hold the speed of the paceline, drop back with the leader—it's okay to sit in the pack when you are new. All riders have experienced this at one time. Just explain that you are a novice; the others will appreciate the information and encourage you to sit in.

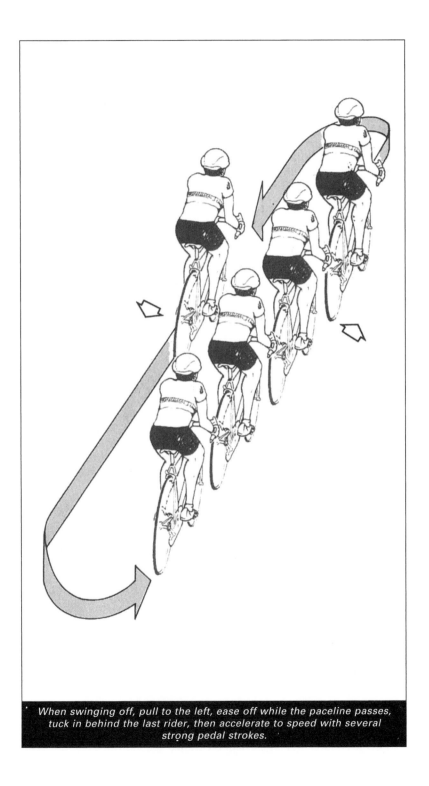

When swinging off, pull to the left, ease off while the paceline passes, tuck in behind the last rider, then accelerate to speed with several strong pedal strokes.

Drafting can be dangerous. One summer when I was riding with a group, we had a strong side wind coming from our right. An experienced and powerful rider was in the lead, taking us out at about 23 mph. After taking her two-minute pull, she dropped off to the left. Due to the strong wind, the proper drafting position was about one foot back and two feet to the left, directly in the path of her retreat. As she slowed, we "crossed front wheels," which means her rear wheel struck my front wheel. The rider in the back always goes down in these instances, and I was no exception. I went down hard, hit my head, rolled onto my face, then shoulder, then hip. The next two riders dodged me and stayed upright.

Knocked unconscious, I awoke to find an ambulance crew loading me into their rescue vehicle and dashing me off to the nearest hospital. A concussion, contusions, and a separated shoulder set my training back a few months, but it was a lesson I won't need to repeat and one I don't want you to experience. Drafting can be dangerous.

Climbing Hills

This may seem hard to believe, but experienced cyclists have a passion for climbing hills. Hills are a measure of cyclists' resolve; they present a personalized challenge, and they allow group riders to break up into smaller packs. If you can develop this passion, you will definitely get strong faster.

The easiest way to climb a hill is to start slowly. If it's a short hill, you can bully your way to the top. But if it's a long hill, shift down at the bottom and spin your way to the top. You should try to hold the same cadence you maintained on the flats, but some hills are just too steep or too long, and you will have to ease down to a 40–65 rpm pedal cadence. If you are forced to shift while climbing, try to do it easily and smoothly. A good rule of thumb is to watch your heart rate: As soon as your heart rate goes up by 5–10 beats, downshift. First, take the tension off the chain by pedaling as lightly as possible and then shift, but not too quickly—you don't want to get your chain jammed into the freewheel.

Practice riding hills. Find a hill that is challenging and work it—do repeat rides up the hill. As you gain strength and confidence, you can try steeper hills and train on them for your repeats.

Your breathing technique on hills is important. During my first year of racing triathlons in Europe, a Frenchman rode up next to me and tried to start a conversation. My high school French just didn't make casual chitchat possible, and I really didn't want to carry on a conversation during a race, when I was using all my oxygen for more important matters. Curiously, he started breathing slower and deeper and gestured as if to demonstrate this to me. I realized then that I was breathing quickly and from the top of my lungs and that he was trying to teach me the correct way to breathe on the uphills. So I tried it—taking deep breaths, with my stomach cavity pushing out as I breathed in. Try this technique; it works.

As you reach the summit of a hill, keep pedaling. As soon as your heart rate drops five beats, upshift. Continue to upshift as you descend and maintain your cadence on the downhill, until you hit the point when you can gain more speed by holding a tightly tucked position than by pedaling. Lower yourself into the tucked position early on the downhill. In the tucked position, your chest is lowered to the handlebars, your knees firmly clutch the top tube, and your elbows are pointed in, with your head lowered.

Climbing out of the Saddle

There are two different times that cyclists climb out of their saddles:

- Racers use this technique to jump ahead of the pack or to break away.
- Riders use this technique to power up hills.

To do either, shift into your middle gears and then stand up onto your pedals. Grasp the brake lever posts, or, if you have aerobars, put both your hands on the handlebars, each hand about three inches from the stem. Using your arms to pull up on the bars, lean your bike alternately left and right at about a 20-degree tilt, over whichever leg is exerting force at any given point. Your leg should be directly over the pedal in this position, which will give you extra power, and the wheels will still track a straight line. Slow your cadence and work the hill, breathing deeply and with control, so that you rhythmically match cadence and breath. Use the technique of climbing out of the saddle on hills as a relief from the grind of sitting in a low gear and slowly working your way to the top. Take advantage of your position to stretch your back.

To win races over uneven terrain, champion cyclists use a combination of both climbing methods, climbing both in and out of the saddle. Remember, standing and climbing not only will break the grind of an uphill but also can power you away from your competition.

Bike Training

Cycling is unique among triathlon events in that it does not take weeks for the person who has recently returned to fitness to become involved in regular workouts. Anyone can start an exercise plan immediately after buying a good bike. Using an indoor training stand for your bike, you can begin with a steady pace, whatever you can maintain comfortably without the distraction of the road conditions or weather. You'll be on your own bike, able to maintain your road riding position, and, what the heck, turn on the TV. Each time a food commercial comes on the tube, do a faster pedal cadence or higher gear until the commercial is over. Unless it's an infomercial for the latest and greatest kitchen appliance or exercise equipment fad, commercials last 30 to 120 seconds. I call this indoor training workout "the McJack," and my recently-returned-to-fitness friends report they are less motivated to stop at fast-food restaurants when they do this workout.

If you live in an area with indoor classes at a nearby club, try one out. A fifty-minute club cycle class is a good approximation of the energy required to finish a 12-mile bike portion of a sprint triathlon. Try to find a club that uses heart rate monitors in the class so the instructor is providing you with verbal instructions that you can adjust to your own fitness

The transition area in Seattle with 4,000 bikes waiting for their riders.

level. "Take it up" could mean all sorts of effort levels, but "Zone 3 for the next 3 minutes" helps keep the group workout individualized for me. Heart cycling covers a variety of techniques (hovers, slides, jumps) that can only be done on a stationary bike but will translate into impressive gains in strength and balance when you head outdoors. In order to push your comfortable limits, you will have to listen to your body through the heart rate monitor feedback.

It's easy for you to build your own training sessions around the indoor trainer or cycle class. You will attain a better spin pace for your everyday cycling and break through to greater fitness. Unfortunately, your bike miles-per-hour speed is measured by a magnet on your front wheel, and that wheel is going nowhere fast on an indoor trainer. You will have to get some road rolling under your bike to prepare for a triathlon. Bike mileage needed to prepare for a triathlon will vary according to your biking experience. As a minimum preparation for a sprint distance of 12 miles, aim for 12–25 miles of continuous aerobic cycling in heart zone 3.

The sample workout schedules that follow will help to get you to the minimum preparation level for the sprint triathlon. Feel free to start at any week that fits your branch of the training tree.

Weeks 1 and 2

WEEKS 1 AND 2	
Monday	Ride 4 miles at a steady pace for about 24 minutes, keeping your heart rate at zone 2, or 65% of your bike max HR.
Tuesday	Rest.
Wednesday	Ride 5 miles at a steady pace, zone 2.
Thursday	Rest and add stretching activity.
Friday	Repeat Monday's routine.
Saturday	Do a longer ride, 8–10 miles but very leisurely, bottom of zone 2, around 70 minutes or between 7–9 mph. Pick up the pace on the second Saturday, however.
Sunday	Rest and add weight training.

Weeks 3 and 4

Once you've been out on the road a bit and are familiar with the terrain available on your bike routes, you should begin to relax and feel comfortable on the bike. Begin to cycle 4 times a week and from 5 to 15 miles at a time.

WEEKS 3 AND 4	
Monday	Ride at a faster pace for 5 miles in 20–25 minutes.
Tuesday	Rest and flexibility-training day.
Wednesday	Try cycling 6 miles in 30–36 minutes at a slghtly slower speed than Monday.
Thursday	Rest and weight-training day.
Friday	Ride 8 miles in 35–48 minutes.
Saturday	This is your long ride day, so increase the distance to 12–15 miles in 60–90 minutes.
Sunday	Rest and flexibility and weight training.

Weeks 5 and 6

Now begin to pick up the cadence and intensity of each workout. You will still be cycling 4 days for about 5–20 miles per day.

WEEKS 5 AND 6	
Monday	Ride 7 miles in about 35 minutes, around 14–16 mph to boost your mileage at a greater speed.
Tuesday	Rest and flexibility and weight training.
Wednesday	Slowing down, cycle 8 miles in 40–48 minutes and enjoy the scenery!
Thursday	Rest and flexibility and weight training.
Friday	Repeat Monday's workout and route.
Saturday	Finish the week with a 20-mile ride at 10–15 mph average, or ride continuously for 90 minutes, whichever you prefer.
Sunday	Rest and flexibility and weight training.

Weeks 7 and 8

Your target is to ride 25 miles continuously, and these are the days when you should be nearing that goal. Ride 5–25 miles, 5 times a week.

WEEKS 7 AND 8	
Monday	Ride 8 miles in 30–40 minutes, around 12–15 mph.
Tuesday	Easy 5 miles in 35 minutes.
Wednesday	Ride 10 miles in 50–60 minutes.
Thursday	Rest and flexibility and weight training.
Friday	Repeat Monday's workout and route.
Saturday	Go for it! Try 25 miles at a pace you feel is comfortable, around 10–13 mph.
Sunday	Rest and flexibility and weight training.

This schedule may be too difficult. If so, cut back. If it's too easy and you can already cycle 25 miles or more, here are some different types of bike workouts that focus either on intervals or on continuous training:

• **_Sprints:_** A maximum effort for short bursts, followed by easy, spinning rest periods. After a long warm-up period, use telephone poles as a marker. Sprint for two poles and rest for three poles. In the beginning, do three to five sets per workout, and later increase both quantity of sets and distance (number) of poles.

• **_Long Intervals:_** These should be 2–4 minutes in duration, with your heart rate rising close to its maximum. Long intervals are on the border between anaerobic and aerobic training. Using time as your gauge, do a "ladder" of progressively longer intervals with 1:1 rest ratios. The first step up the ladder is 2 minutes "on" (riding as hard as you can in heart zone 4), followed by 2 minutes "off" (easy spinning for recovery in zone 3). The next step is 3 minutes on and 3 minutes off. The final step up the ladder is 4 minutes of hard riding, followed by 4 minutes of rest riding. Next, go down the ladder using the reverse order.

• **_Anaerobic Threshold Training:_** This is a medium-intensity level of training, from 4–30 minutes in length. Set a continuous speed (using your cyclometer) that is difficult but not impossible to maintain for the duration of the workout. Let's say that you ride your long intervals (2–4 minutes) at 19 mph. For anaerobic threshold training, you would back down from this speed to 16–17 mph.

• **_LSD:_** Long slow distances are relaxed endurance workouts at 65–75 percent of your maximum heart rate (zones 2 and 3), for as long as you want to ride (beyond 30 minutes). You are at aerobic training levels, and the pace is relatively easy.

Hundreds of other bike-training workouts are available that you can use in your systematic training schedule. An excellent resource is the second edition of _The Heart Rate Monitor Book for Cyclists_ (VeloPress, 2002), which Sally Reed and I co-authored. Design workouts yourself—it's part of the fun. You can also join bike-training groups and discover what other cyclists find most beneficial, and meet some more training partners.

Susan Booher finishing strong and with proper running form in the Avon, an international all-women's running series.

BASIC MOVES FOR RUNNING

Run Biomechanics

Running is the art of fluid forward propulsion, driven by the synchronization of all of your body's parts, up to and including the mental one.

Efficient running is based upon economy of motion. When you run economically, like a car you will get more miles per gallon of energy, and your engine will run with fewer breakdowns and with less wear and tear. This is the ideal running form, starting from the top and going down:

Head: Your chin is up, and your eyes look forward at least ten feet, preferably toward the horizon. Breathing is through your mouth, and your jaw and face are so relaxed that they might bounce as you run.

Shoulders: They are relaxed and parallel to the ground.

Arms: Bent 90 degrees at the elbows (which are within one inch of your waist), your arms rotate freely in an arc that projects forward and backward, not rotationally around your axis. Your hands should not cross your center line (that imaginary line from your nose, through your navel, to your feet), and the swinging of your arms should allow them to freely cut a course between your hipbone and bustline.

Hands: Your wrists are straight and pointing forward, while your hands are loosely cupped with the thumb and third finger touching (no clenched fists). Your palms should face inward toward each other.

Back: The spine is upright and erect, neither leaning forward nor arching back, but instead is straight and perpendicular to the ground. If a string were attached to the back of your head, your back would be touching it along its entire length.

Chest: Your chest is lifted up, as if a rope attached to your sternum is pulling you forward. Your chest actually leads the way as you run.

Hips: The pelvis is tucked under and your hips are also pushed forward. If you were to put your hands on your buttocks and push them forward, you would feel your shoulders, head, and hips all line up.

Legs: Again, your limbs should be moving in a forward and backward direction, with no rotation around your central axis (the vertical line extending through the center of your body). Keep your feet low to the ground, with little back-kick (unless you are sprinting—sprinters need the power

Correct Running Form

achieved through high knees and long stride lengths). Faster running is accomplished by increases in stride frequency, so the shorter the stride, the more strides you can take and the faster you will go.

Feet: Land quietly and softly with little sound on impact, and take care that your stride length is comfortable and not over-extended. Land on your heels first and roll forward off your toes; the only time your toes strike first is if you are sprinting. Your feet should cut a course directly underneath you, not out to the sides.

One of the best ways to check your form is to watch yourself run as you pass the glass windows of storefronts. You should see the efficient conversion of all energy to forward motion.

The best way to learn to run efficiently is to practice and develop a running style in which all body motion is in a straight, forward direction. There should be no side-to-side action, and gravity should keep you low to the ground.

When you run efficiently, you should feel light and quick—it's a feeling of prancing, not lumbering. Practice breathing deeply (also called "belly breathing"), as your breaths should be full, not shallow or from the top of your lungs.

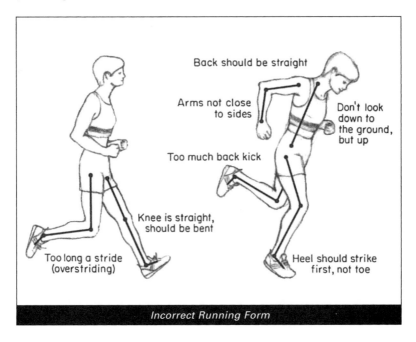

Back should be straight

Arms not close to sides

Don't look down to the ground, but up

Too much back kick

Knee is straight, should be bent

Too long a stride (overstriding)

Heel should strike first, not toe

Incorrect Running Form

Changing your running form is like changing your signature—it's something you must constantly practice. Dedicate one day a week to training in your new efficient form, and work on it so hard that it becomes imprinted as your new signature.

When you have it down, efficient running is like being on cruise control—you can just set the form and the speed and run effortlessly for what seems like forever.

Run Training

For run training, keep in mind the concepts of aerobic and anaerobic training, discussed in Chapter 2 on heart zones training. Following is a list of different training methods commonly used by runners, divided into continuous training methods and interval training. In Chapters 6, 7, and 8, you will see how to combine these methods into your own personalized training program.

Steady State Training

Aerobic Runs

The training period lasts 30–60 minutes and is usually at a light intensity level, such as a five-mile, easy, steady-state run. An aerobic run will help with your strength and endurance.

A great way to get in this workout is to do a steady-state heart rate test, as discussed in the heart zones training chapter. Warm up for 5–10 minutes, then run one mile at a steady heart rate (pick the middle of your aerobic zone, or 75 percent of your max HR). Time yourself. This gives you a baseline speed against which you can test your improvement. After several weeks of training, you should be able to run the same distance at the same heart rate with a faster time.

Long Slow Distance (LSD)

These are submaximal workouts performed at a very low intensity over a very long distance, which are also known as "over-distance" training. Usually, the pace of an LSD workout is slower than your racing speed by at least a minute per mile. The purpose here is to develop long-distance endurance.

Run for 1–3 hours (5–20 miles) at a lower level of intensity. Your target heart rate for this is zone 2, or about 60–70 percent of your max HR. Try to maintain the steady easy pace throughout the run.

*Every woman is capable of completing a triathlon—
every size, every shape, every age.*

Time Trials

This run is for a specific distance, at a constant strong intensity, that is timed and used to measure improvement. Time trials are also called pace training, because they teach the triathlete proper pacing. This type of workout will increase your strength and speed.

Interval Training

Anaerobic Intervals

This training involves an intense effort over a relatively short period of time, commonly from 30 seconds to 2 minutes. You are stressing your anaerobic system by a near-maximal output. A 1-mile bike time trial and a 400-meter run (one lap around a track) are anaerobic interval distances. Anaerobic intervals work you on both strength and speed.

Run for a total of 1–5 miles, sprinting for up to 2 minutes and then resting for the same amount of time.

Anaerobic Threshold Intervals

This is an interval that lasts from 4 to 30 minutes and is of high intensity. Doing this type of workout will increase your anaerobic power, important for racing.

Fartlek

Literally translated, fartlek means "speed play." It's a method of training in which there are relatively long-duration, high-intensity periods mixed with low-intensity training (which serve as rest periods), but you still do a continuous workout overall. Fartleks are designed to increase your strength and to help you have fun with your running and keep you interested in your training and activities.

Run 3 miles, running for 30 seconds then walking for 60 seconds, for the whole distance. You can mix up the amount of time you do for each repeat; it doesn't have to be consistent (that's why it's called "speed play"). Your heart rate should go up and down between zone 3 (aerobic zone) during the runs and zone 2 (temperate zone) when you're walking. Remember to warm up for at least 5 minutes before, and give yourself enough time afterward to cool down.

Long Intervals

This involves work periods of 2–15 minutes with intermittent rest periods during the interval. The length of time for the rest is such that you can maintain each of the repeats at a constant rate during the training period. Rest time in long-interval training is usually 2–5 minutes. Do this work to increase your endurance.

Resistance Repeats

These are interval repetitions using a form of resistance for increased workload, such as running up hills (with the rest period being the downhill), running in sand, or running using weights. These workouts help your leg strength and get you accustomed to running in various conditions.

Sprints

These involve maximal effort of 10–30 seconds, such as a 100-meter run or 200-meter bike sprint. This activity increases your speed.

TRAIN, DON'T EXERCISE—
GET EXCITED

Allez. Allez. Allez. Allez.

The French shouted these words at the top of their voices as I raced over the Alps and through their cobblestone streets during the Nice Triathlon.

Faido. Faido. Faido. Faido.

The Japanese chanted this rhythmically as I raced through rice paddies and over their narrow macadam streets at the Ironman in Japan.

These words are buried in the center of my brain. I use them frequently when I race and train, for they now have special motivational meaning for me.

Allez means "let's go." And "go," for the French, is a single word that combines two powerful English words, that all athletes, regardless of sex or race, instinctively use—"go" and "power."

Faido, on the other hand, means "to fight."

Let me explain. As I raced toward the finish line of the Ironman in Japan, the polite Japanese spectators applauded and yelled *faido.* I thought the word meant "second," since that was my position in the field. At the finish line, I asked an English-speaking Japanese triathlete what *faido* meant.

She startled me with her answer, since "fighting" was not in my athletic vocabulary; it made me think of doing damage to others. She saw my confusion

As she leaves T2, this Danskin triathlete is fulfilling the Danskin slogan "The woman who starts the race is not the same as the woman who finishes it."

and said, " 'To fight' to a Japanese means to fight against that inner part of yourself that prevents you from doing your best."

Now I use *allez* whenever I need a boost and *faido* whenever I'm working against myself.

You, too, can use these buzzwords to keep going beyond that first step, those first few weeks of participation in triple fitness. In the beginning, we are easily motivated by health benefits: toned muscles, girth reductions, increased stamina, and cardiovascular improvements. But after the beginning, once you have settled into a routine, you may forget why you began tri-training and wonder why you are putting yourself through so much trouble. In that case, think about the meaning of *faido,* and say *allez* aloud. Let's go!

Exercise Versus Training

Exercise is defined as bodily or mental exertion. Training is to make proficient by instruction and practice (from *Random House Webster's College Dictionary,* 1991). Someone who exercises does it usually for the purpose of getting or staying in shape. A person who trains has a greater goal in mind, achieving a dream. To me a dream is a goal with a finish banner. What counts is that you set goals and accomplish them.

A woman new to running might train with the goal of running her first 5K race. An Ironwoman trains with the goal of testing everything she has in the most grueling one-day race around. Exercise is a part of training, but it isn't the whole thing or even the most important. If you pick a goal, you have a purpose that will get you out training even when you don't feel like it. You are an athlete. An athlete in my playbook is anyone who trains.

Examples of goals you could set:
Why do you want to do a triathlon?

Because I want to get back into shape.

Because it gives me motivation to reach for a goal.

Because my friends are training for it.

What's your motivation for doing a triathlon?

I love to be outdoors.

I find new challenges exciting.

I need to exercise to feel better about myself.

What might be obstacles to doing a triathlon?

I don't know how.

I am scared and I might not finish.

I've never done anything like this before.

I don't have time to add one more activity to my lifestyle.

List the specific short-term or long-term goal that you have set:

To finish with a smile of joy on my face.

To get back into shape and stay in shape so I can do my best.

To beat the clock—the time I have planned on finishing the race.

To help my friend finish.

The spokes of the training wheel (discussed later in this chapter) are the training plan. Each spoke represents a new phase of training. That is, training needs to be progressive so that you get fit first and then fitter and fitter.

To determine how many weeks to spend in each training phase, count back from the date of your event and determine the number of weeks you need.

The number of weeks of training for the triathlon is ____ weeks.

The Training Program

To use a down-to-earth metaphor, training for triathlons is like preparing, ingesting, and recovering from a major meal. It involves a recipe, ingredients, preparation time, equipment, planning time, labor, measurements, the actual event (eating the meal), cleanup, and rest afterward. Throughout the training program, as in cooking a meal, there are multiple activities occurring —different pans on the stove at the same time. Welcome to the gourmet training experience!

Like a good meal, tri-training is especially pleasurable because there is variety among its courses. Each training course or discipline, whether swim, bike, or run, presents its own unique experiences and challenges, yet training systems that work on one course will apply to the other two. The courses and the obstacles they present vary, but the training system remains the same. Like a well-planned meal, each course complements the next, and all work together toward a spectacular finish!

I am commonly asked by first-timers (and multi-timers) two questions:

Why train and why compete in trisports?

How much training do I really need to do well?

You may have the same questions as well, so I'll address them right now.

Why Begin Tri-Training?

Many women who do the Danskin Women's Triathlon come to the race out of a desire to lose weight and get in shape. I tell these women that they shouldn't be focusing on the negative idea of losing weight; they should focus on the positive concept of gaining fitness. To gain fitness, you need a goal, one that goes outside of yourself. Losing weight is a goal, but isn't it better to focus on something you become rather than something you lose? Completing your first triathlon is a great goal, and one that can lead you into a whole new idea of yourself. Repeatedly I see women who thought they could never accomplish something like a triathlon make their way to the finish line at the Danskin. Finishing is winning, and on the way you gain fitness and pride in yourself and your achievement.

Probably the clearest way I can explain it is to describe an experience I had during the same Ironman race in Japan that taught me about *faido*. As I reached the turnaround point on the 112-mile bike leg, I saw a banner stretched across the road, the only English banner among the hundreds the Japanese had placed along the route.

The banner bore three short words that struck me with the force of a thousand. Their brevity had such an impact that I will carry them with me for the rest of my life.

The banner read "Do Your Best."

As a woman in triathlon, that's what I want. And that's what I want for you.

How Much Training to Complete a Triathlon?

Training for triathlons is a cyclic process. This cycle of training is called the "training wheel" because it resembles the wheel on your bike. A bike wheel is designed for strength, balance, and rotation. This training program has the same construction with spokes that divide each of the different phases into distinct parts. And, like a bike wheel, the spokes of the training wheel serve as the dividers that separate and distinguish each part of your personalized training program for your first triathlon.

In the center of the training wheel is the hub. Again, like a bike wheel, this hub is the center, the focus, the connection piece that each spoke threads through. Symbolically, the hub might best represent your training goals. In many ways, it is the hub that is the center point, the point of it all.

The rim of the training wheel represents time, that all too precious commodity that is free to all of us and yet one of our greatest treasures. Time is also an equalizer: Everyone has the same amount of time in every single day. It is what you do with your time and how you manage it that the training wheel system guides you through. You will spend less time training; you will get more benefit from your training time.

Unlike a bike wheel and as the diagram here shows, each of the spokes is not spaced equally apart. There are different lengths of time you spend between spokes depending in large part on your individual needs and goals. If you are new to triathlon training, spend more time in the first two spokes: base and skills. But if you are a seasoned veteran, you probably have a well-established base and can choose to begin with the second or third spoke. In that case, spend more time in the other three phases: strength or hills, intervals or speed work, and power, which are the combination of all the spokes.

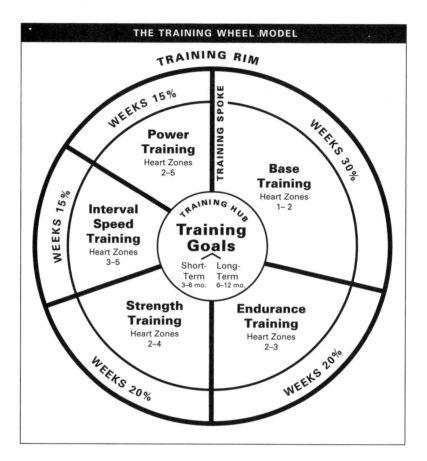

THE TRAINING WHEEL MODEL

TRAINING RIM

WEEKS 15%

TRAINING SPOKE

Power Training
Heart Zones 2–5

WEEKS 30%

Base Training
Heart Zones 1–2

WEEKS 15%

Interval Speed Training
Heart Zones 3–5

TRAINING HUB

Training Goals

Short-Term 3–6 mo. Long-Term 6–12 mo.

Strength Training
Heart Zones 2–4

Endurance Training
Heart Zones 2–3

WEEKS 20%

WEEKS 20%

Sample Training Wheel

To construct a training wheel, first you need to build the hub. Answer these questions to set the center point of your triathlon training. You can write your answers here or in your training log, or pin them up on your refrigerator to help keep you motivated.

- Why do you want to do a triathlon?
- What is your motivation for doing a triathlon?
- What might be obstacles or what might get in the way of your doing a triathlon?
- What is your specific short-term or long-term goal?

The sample training wheel shown here assumes that your goal is to participate in a triathlon in six weeks.

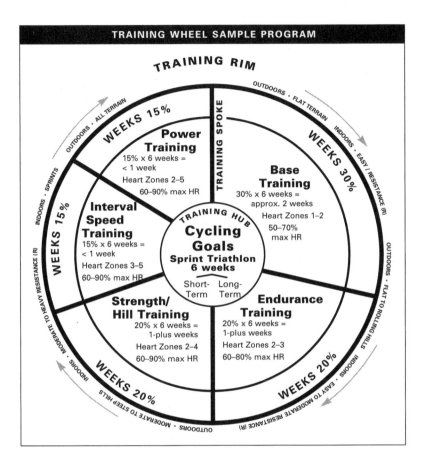

TRAINING WHEEL SAMPLE PROGRAM

Adjust this sample triathlon training program to make it fit your individual situation. It needs to account for the amount of time you have available, your current fitness level, and your motivation. Also, training is a blend of art and science. Use your double-action heart to create this training program: your emotional heart with its intuitive and creative action and your physical heart with its physical pumping action.

Training is also a series of workouts that create physiological stress followed by a period of recovery. This repeat of stress and recovery creates the fitness phenomenon called the "training effect." That is what you are doing by training in different spokes during this six-week or longer period: improving your fitness.

One key point is to change your training as you gain fitness. By moving from one spoke on the training wheel to the next, you get fitter. As you become fit, the workouts get easier, you get better, and your training heart

Identify what you love and fill your life with it.

rates at the same intensities will improve (get lower). Using a heart rate monitor is a must for reaching your fittest.

In the five different spokes surrounding your training hub—your goals —you will be adding different types of workouts. Here is a description of the five spokes and reference to the training workouts that you should incorporate into each.

Base and Skill Training Spoke

This spoke emphasizes getting to the basics: swim, bike, and run technique and cardio fitness. Workouts are short in length or time. This spoke is described as "easy, low heart zone, short distance" training. All the training is in the low heart zones: zones 1–3. (For more information, refer to *Heart Zone Training.*) The workouts are fun, easy, and aerobic. This is your base period. Train here for approximately 2 weeks. Each week you will be building your cardiovascular aerobic system. Work on improving your biomechanics or technique of running, swimming, and cycling. Ask a friend to look at your technique and make suggestions so you can become more efficient.

Frequency: 3 workouts per week: 1 swim, 1 bike, and 1 run.

Intensity: Heart zone 1, healthy heart; heart zone 2, temperate; heart zone 3, aerobic.

Time: 15–30 minutes per workout. Total for the week: 45 minutes– 1.5 hours.

Endurance Spoke

Now that you have developed your base aerobic capacity, it is time to train for longer periods, slightly harder, and to push the heart rate intensity. Building a bigger and more powerful base leads to building your aerobic foundation. Your goal is to develop muscular endurance during this training period.

Frequency: 3–4 workouts per week: 1 swim, 1 bike, and 1–2 runs.

Intensity: Heart zone 1, healthy heart; heart zone 2, temperate; heart zone 3, aerobic.

Time: 15–35 minutes per workout. Total for the week: 45 minutes–1.75 hours.

Note: Change your workout routine to include one endurance workout. To do this, pick one of the three sports and do one workout that is longer than you have ever trained before. Make that a 35-minute or more training session at low heart rates. This builds your endurance capacity overall.

Strength Spoke

This training cycle is the period when you will be working on developing muscle strength. Strength is your muscle's ability to generate force against

Left to right, Cameron Sweeny, Sally Edwards, and Maggie Sullivan, organizers of the Danskin Triathlon.

resistance. In short, you want to give your sport-specific muscles more strength and power. The best way to do this is to train with resistance: on hills, into the wind, with overload of weight, using swimming aids in the pool, on a treadmill with elevation, and the like.

Frequency: 4–5 workouts per week: 1 swim, 1 bike, and 1 run, plus 1–2 workouts in your sport that needs the most improvement.

Intensity: Heart zones 1–3.

Time: 15–45 minutes per workout. Total for the week: 45 minutes–2 hours.

Note: Keep the once-a-week endurance workout and extend it to 40 minutes. Add 1 new workout to build strength such as riding hills on your bike once a week.

Interval/Speed Spoke

One of the best ways to improve speed is to train using repeats or sets of short periods of time going faster than normal. This is called interval training. Interval training is one of the most important times to use your heart rate monitor because you will be riding in higher heart zones. Higher-intensity training improves your recovery ability and your ability to sustain higher heart rates that you might experience during the triathlon.

Frequency: 5 workouts per week: 1 swim, 2 bike, and 1 run plus 1 interval training session

Intensity: Heart zones 1–3 or 1–4.

Time: 15–50 minutes per workout. Total for the week: 75 minutes–2 hours.

Note: Keep one endurance, one strength, and now add one speed or interval workout during this week. For example: swim one endurance, bike one strength, bike one endurance, and run one interval workout during the week. The fourth workout can be an aerobic training session (heart zones 1–3) in your sport that needs the most improvement.

Power Spoke

During this last week before the triathlon, you will add a "brick" to your week. A brick is a swim-bike or a bike-run; it is two sports in one workout. Practice your transitions and try to time them.

Frequency: 5–6 workouts per week: 1–2 swims, 1–2 bike, and 1–2 runs plus 1 brick.

What? I'm not a size 8?

Intensity: Heart zones 1–4.

Time: 15–60 minutes per workout. Total for the week: 80 minutes–3 hours.

Note: Bricks are fun. Do them with a training buddy. If you can, try both a swim-bike and bike-run on different days. Try the distances of the race during your training this week: swim 1 km (1,090 yards) on your swim day. Bike 12 miles on your bike day. Run 5 km (3.1 miles) on your run day. Do a brick on your brick day, but keep the distances shorter than race distances if you want.

The process of change to becoming a triathlete proceeds step by step. The first step is to learn. Read, ask questions, keep a training log, ask for help, join a training group such as the Danskin Mentor-Mentee program, get a personal trainer, or sign up for an e-coach. The second step is determination and conviction. Set a goal and a plan that is from the heart. The third step is action: train. And finally, the fourth step and my favorite is effort. It is the effort to stay on a triathlon training program that you created, that fits into your life, and that works for you.

And if you ever need encouragement, always know that I am behind you supporting you in your training and racing. After all, the winner is the one who has the most fun.

The feeling of accomplishment and joy is expressed as Sally Edwards crosses the finish line of the 1984 Women's Olympic Marathon trials.

TRAIN, DON'T EXERCISE— GET INSPIRED

Welcome to the union of fit women who have passed the first hurdle of lifetime athleticism—the novice or beginner stage. You have promoted yourself to the class of tri-women who have made a commitment to the sport and who are taking their level of experience to new heights.

You are in the middle of an evolutionary process: from the excitement of trying your first triathlon, to being inspired to make triathlon a part of your life. As you approach each higher level, new parameters to training will be added. You will also need to understand more of the training principles and have a higher level of appreciation for the intricacies of performance training.

As a beginner, you were testing the triathletic waters. You may have been approaching training gingerly, working out for the purpose of gaining fitness and managing weight, and looking to comfortably finish a first-timer event like the Danskin. You have now hit the point where you've realized that training has purpose. This is the level where you make the transition from saying "Yes, I've done a triathlon" to "I am training for an improved (something)." The word "for" indicates that you have intent. Let me show you. Get something to write with, and don't read any further until you have a writing utensil in hand.

Clarifying Values and Personalizing your Goals

Values are those things on which we are willing to spend resources—time, effort, money. Values exist in all areas of your life, and their priorities change over time. They motivate us, determine our focus, and determine how we feel when we are done. Start from the heart, taking responsibility for where you are right now and answer these questions for yourself.

1. Identify: Why do I do what I do?

2. Clarify the value: How do I know when I'm ...?

What does _____ mean to me?

What causes me to feel_____?

3. Rank your values in order of importance.

Ask: If I had _____, would it be OK not to have_____?

Now, fill in the blanks below by answering this question:

What do I want to accomplish from training?

1. I am training for _____

2. I am also training for _____

3. I would like to train for _____

Stop. If you decided to pass by those three statements, you made a mistake. Go back and fill them in now. It is important that you do that before you read the next paragraph—please.

The "training for" further separates the trainers from the exercisers, because it means that you have a goal, and that you want to accomplish something. If you are into fitness for staying in shape, then you are a member of the exercise community. However, if you are into fitness for accomplishing something—learning more about yourself, meeting new friends, expanding your horizons, entering a race, or beating a nemesis—then you train, you don't exercise.

As you take the steps from excited to inspired to ignited, you put aside exercise and learn about new training principles such as

- Large and small goals
- The four cycles: annual, seasonal, monthly, and weekly
- The power of the distance training methods

Together, these principles will lead you into your own individualized training schedule.

Large and Small Goals

Remember, goals are what help separate a trainer from an exerciser. Your large goals are what you wrote as your "training for" answers, and they will help you determine the framework of your macro cycles. But there are also small goals, sometimes called objectives, that are the steps to accomplishing the large goals, and these are what micro cycles focus on.

However, I firmly believe the large goal is what you always need to focus upon. It's like having an elephant in your garden, trampling your violets. You could work on completing a small goal—protecting your violets—by fencing the flowers off with chicken wire. However, since elephants aren't chickens, that probably won't work very well. What would work would be to focus on your large goal—getting rid of the elephant—by calling your local zoo. To put it briefly, give your attention to the elephants in your life, and your violets will grow beautifully.

The Four Cycles: Annual, Seasonal, Monthly, and Weekly

1. The annual cycle *is a forest of heart zones training trees,* numerous and varied, that you climb over a one-year period of training and training goals.

2. The seasonal cycles *are periods of two to eight months duration that together form an annual cycle.* Think of the seasonal cycle as a wreath made up of the branches of heart zones training trees. There are six stages to a seasonal cycle.

3. Monthly (macro) cycles *are four-week training periods that focus on one stage of the seasonal cycle.* The monthly cycle stage roughly corresponds to spokes on a heart zones training wheel.

4. Weekly cycles *are seven-day training periods, four to a monthly cycle,* that are planned using heart zones training workload points and principles.

Annual Cycle

The annual cycle is probably the most difficult to formulate because it requires you to look into the future. Still, I believe if you've done your interior work on clarifying your values and goals, the exterior planning will be much easier. To design an annual cycle, you need to answer this question: Athletically, what would I like to accomplish this year and the next year?

An annual cycle gives you the opportunity to plan your athletics over the long term. An example of an annual cycle would be to set your first year of training as a learning experience, one in which you would like to finish one triathlon. In your second annual cycle, you might like to train and enter five triathlons of both sprint and international distance and complete a century bike ride. In year three, you might want to finish a long-course triathlon and attempt your first marathon.

Jot down a few annual goals that may have occurred to you as you read this chapter. Be ambitious. Put your heart on your sleeve and spark your imagination. You can look them over later and analyze their appropriateness. Let's fly a little for now!

ANNUAL CYCLE				
G	Year	200__	200__	200__
O	1			
A	2			
L	3			
S	4			

Picture the annual cycle as a number of heart zones training wheels, each balanced and true, waiting for your feet to find the pedals and your leg muscles to power them.

Seasonal Cycle

These cycles, usually two to eight months long, are the big pictures in performance training, your maps of your large training goals and timelines. Some triathletes draw a training map based on seasons of the year: spring, summer, fall, and winter, making four seasonal cycles. Others prefer to divide their year into as many as seven seasonal cycles, based on their racing schedules.

I am a two-season cycler: Eight months of the year I race in triathlons, and four months of the year I run in road races or adventure races. Seasonal cycles are usually two to eight months in length and are individually tailored to your type of athleticism.

Get a big year-at-a-glance wall calendar. Put all events on it—your birthday, anniversary, mammogram appointment, car pool days, school vacations —all dates, important or otherwise. For example, you should note dates you plan for recuperation, travel, specific races you have scheduled, and the sports activities you will be training for. Give yourself the gift of time and divide the months of the year up, based on what you want to accomplish. Honesty is the best policy. All this should begin to give you an idea of how to set up your year-long seasonal cycle plan. Jot down the highlights here:

SEASONAL CYCLE PLAN FOR THIS YEAR	
January	
February	
March	
April	
May	
June	
July	
August	
September	
October	
November	
December	

Imagine the seasonal cycle as a collection of different length boughs you are weaving together to make a continuous wreath of fitness performance.

Monthly (Macro) Cycles

Monthly (or macro) cycles are periods of time, generally of four to ten weeks, within each seasonal cycle. Macro cycles are usually dedicated to improving one major factor of your performance—for example, speed. A series of macro cycles will form a progression, from base training to post-race recovery, which, when united, form a full seasonal cycle.

In March 1992, I started my season with a goal of training for completion of four Ironmans, aspiring to set the master's world record in all four. I did just that because I followed this training program. After the Ironman World Championships in October, I needed a rest macro cycle, so I gave myself an eleven-week macro cycle to rest, until January 1.

The Six Macro Cycles for Intermediate Triathletes

Training is a progression—a series of little steps that lead you to the completion of your goals. Whatever your seasonal training goal, the little steps needed to get there are the six different macro cycles: base, skills, intensity, peak, competition, and recovery.

Base Macro Cycle: 2 weeks–2 months (2–8 weeks)

This is a cycle of low intensity and low training volume, when you lay the foundation of your training program. Exercise physiologists call this the "aerobic buildup phase," because you are training for the aerobic, not the anaerobic, component of fitness. The cycle consists of workouts that are easy and continuous and that lead to strength and stamina, not necessarily speed, although you will need to introduce some speed work into the later macro cycle weeks. This is also a stage of developing strength, so include weight workouts with machines or free weights as well as sport-specific strength workouts, such as running and cycling hills.

Skills Macro Cycle: 1 month (2–4 weeks)

This is a cycle of sport-specific training, for the purpose of improving your technique. It is a time to fine-tune your swim, bike, and run biomechanics—to concentrate on developing the movement skills more than the endurance skills. Attending a sport-specific weekend such as the one directed by Jazz

It was a great day! This forty-two-year-old had completed her first triathlon and said, "I think I talk more about that one day in my life than any other, except my wedding."

Scheingraber at Camp Danskin is fun and can hugely impact this stage of your training. Camp Danskin is suitable for all fitness levels because the workouts are based on the principles of heart zones training designed to let you go as hard or easy as your plan might require. At Camp Danskin, the concentration is on skills and practice. Here's a basic day: morning walk or run (shower), breakfast, technical lecture or visualization workshop, snack, swim/bike/run workout (shower), lunch, skills and drills workout, snack, lecture, dinner, lecture, and then to bed.

It's a true camp; locations are chosen for their serene beauty, open-water practice opportunity, comfortable accommodations, and great chow. Because studying the mechanics of sports really does lead to enhanced biomechanical efficiency, you'll want to schedule in a weekend with the women at Camp Danskin. Or join a club or enhance your skills with the aid of a local expert. Find these local experts and keep going to them as you would to your hairstylist. Approximately 80 percent of your training volume during this cycle will be aerobic and over-distance training.

Intensity Macro Cycle: 2–4 months (8–16 weeks)

This is a demanding and vigorous cycle. You take the base and skills you've developed over the prior two macro cycles and add intensity training. This period will usually include the highest training volume of any macro cycle. Approximately 50–60 percent of your training volume will still be LSD, aerobic training, and aerobic time trials. The balance needs to be in interval training, such as time trials, fartleks, resistance repeats, and anaerobic intervals. This is a time to enter an individual sport race such as a 5K road race or a bike time trial.

Peak Macro Cycle: 2–4 months (8–16 weeks)

This is a short macro cycle built around sharpening workouts, which are characterized by lower-distance training at higher-intensity volumes. Physiologically, you are stressing your energy systems at high speeds in order to gain speed, as well as to refine your technique. Some coaches refer to this as sharpening. It is also called peaking because the decrease in training volume allows you to store more energy in preparation for a big race, yet it is a sharpening because of the refinement component.

Competition Macro Cycle: 1–4 months (4–16 weeks)

This is the cycle when you are capable of racing at your best. I think of it as the dessert of training, because it is such a delicious stage to a competitive athlete. Over half the training during this cycle will be over-distance training, and this is a time to train actively while in the midst of a racing schedule and what it entails (travel, diet changes, psychological stress). Maintaining your aerobic base should be central to your planning. Interval training should represent 10–15 percent of the training volume.

Recovery Macro Cycle: 1–4 months (4–16 weeks)

This is the rest phase of training, when you can slow down. Training in this cycle is of very low intensity and moderate to low volume. It is a stage when sport-specific training is unimportant; take up new activities such as cross-country skiing, in-line skating, or aerobic dancing. It is an active restoration period—you might enjoy playing team sports like volleyball or softball and work on your team-playing skills. Enjoy the recovery macro cycle and stay active.

Weekly Training Plan

Throughout this book, I've discussed the individualization of effort through the use of a heart rate monitor. I explained the training wheel and discussed some self-testing you can do to place yourself on a spoke in it. The weekly plan that you write for your life and your athletic workload is your way of fine-tuning, of "trueing," your wheel.

You established your seasonal schedule when you answered the questions about what you are training for. To accomplish your monthly cycle goals and travel around the training wheel, you must design a systematic training program. This program must be a written record of a number of indicators and factors. You design your own training schedules because training is an individualized program—what works for you works only for you, not for anyone else.

As an example, a swim coach writes a workout for her team to perform. On the team of thirty swimmers, three are stars, and the remainder perform adequately but not as well. Why? There are a number of reasons, but probably the first is that the coach has designed a training program that is working for only those three swimmers; the other twenty-seven need a different program—one that works for them.

For you to create your training program, you will need a way to write it down: a sample format, a worksheet, a template, an outline. You already have most of the information that you need to fill in the blanks; what you are missing is the swim-bike-run workout for each individual training day.

I know that writing your weekly training program is not easy. You might be hesitating, not putting pen to paper for fear of over-committing or underachieving. Start somewhere. I guarantee that a systematic training program like this achieves two major goals: You get the most out of your training, and you do it in the least amount of time. If you dedicate the time to planning your schedule, the return is enormous. Isn't it better to wake up in the morning and know what you are planning to do for the day? Part of your plan is to have fun, so don't stress out by wondering what to do today. Plan a week's worth of workouts in advance. Make it fit into your monthly cycle. Fill in the blanks in your training plan. Complete the form, weekly tri-training planner, on pages 80–81.

Training Log

The purpose of the triathlon log shown here is to keep a record of the training you have completed, both quantitatively and qualitatively. In other words, you can use the triathlon log as your private training diary—you can admit to your problems and your revelations, workouts missed, difficulties encountered, and personal records set.

You can purchase copies of the triathlon log by visiting my website www.heartzone.com.

How Much Training Do You Need?

You may still be wondering how much is too much, how little is too little. I can honestly say that this information will come only with consistent use of a log and your honest commitment to monitoring your workload. Recording results in key areas such as heart rate, hours of sleep, body fat, distance, and the rest is crucial to your balanced approach to achieving better performance and fitness.

Maybe you are under the impression or you've read that there is a formula all endurance athletes or women triathlon greats have used to compete effectively and stay healthy. In fact, no such formula exists. Training is specific and individual to you. I've entered my fifth decade on this planet and my third decade as a professional athlete, and still I plan for my goals, log every key indicator, and review my plan. If you want to get something done, measure it; if you want to get something done well, record it.

Training Volume

Your total yearly training volume will depend on what you want to accomplish and what your goals are. It also depends on a realistic appraisal of the time you have available and how well you are able to manage the time you have. Answer this question: On average, how much time do I have each day to train? Then multiply that number times the number of days per week and the number of weeks per year that you are going to train, and you have your annual volume.

Total Yearly = _____ x _____ x _____
Training Volume = average hours/day x number of days/week x number of weeks/year

The numbers could look something like this:
1 hour/day x 6 days/week x 52 weeks = 312 hours/year

YEARLY TRAINING VOLUME (HOURS)				
Proficiency Level	Triathlete	Runner	Swimmer	Cyclist
Professional	800–1,400	500–700	400–600	700–1,200
Competitor	400–800	300–500	300–400	350–700
Intermediate	300–400	200–300	200–300	200–350
Beginner	< 300	< 200	< 200	< 200

Use the chart to compare your yearly volume with that of other athletes of different proficiency levels.

The Power of the Distance Training Methods

The amount of cross-training you'll need to perform depends upon your goals and skills, and how motivated you've been by races such as the Danskin. So, on a very subtle, personal level, I can't presume to tell you how much to train. However, there is an easy formula you can use to find the approximate training volume you will need: Take the lengths of the event in which you wish to compete and make your training distances a multiple of the racing distances.

For example, the Danskin Triathlon Series has distances of 1K swim, 20K bike, and 5K run, which are the standard lengths for a sprint triathlon. Just because the distances are short doesn't mean that the race is easy; most women trade the shorter distances for faster speeds, so the effort remains demanding—especially if this is your second time!

Next, take a multiplying factor and apply it to those distances. I've used three as the multiplier in this example, the level of an experienced beginner. To determine your weekly training volume, multiply the sprint distances by three, and that will equal your weekly training distance.

Formula: Multiple	x	Distances	=	Total Distance to Train per Week
3	x	1K swim	=	3K swim per week
3	x	20K bike	=	60K bike per week
3	x	5K run	=	15K run per week

This is called the "power of the distance" training system. Using the power of the distance, your total weekly volume would be 3 kilometers (just

				Time in Zone				
Date	Sport Activity	Distance	Time	Z1	Z2	Z3	Z4	Z5
Weekly Summary								
Year-to-Date Summary								

WEEKLY TRI-TRAINING PLANNER

Key Workout Type	Average	AM Heart Rate	Body Weight/ Fat	Altimeter	Weight Training Time	Stretching Time	A, B C, F Rating	HZT Points

WEEKLY TRI-TRAINING PLANNER

under 2 miles) of swimming, 60 kilometers (37 miles) on your bike, and 15 kilometers (9 miles) of running.

How much time would it take you to train at the power of three? Calculate the time and see if you can fit it into the amount of time you have available.

The easiest way is to break these distances into parts and time the parts, and then multiply the result by the total distance. For example, if you can swim 100 meters in 2 minutes, then swimming 3,000 meters per week (30 times as far) would take you 60 minutes a week (30 times as long).

Swim: _____minutes per 100 meters x 30 = _____minutes
Bike: _____kilometers per hour divided into 60 kilometers = _____minutes
Run: _____minutes per kilometer x 15 kilometers = _____minutes

Here's an example for a novice triathlete. Does she have enough time in a week to train at the level of the power of three?

Swim: 2 minutes x 30 = 60 minutes
Bike: 26 kilometers per hour divided into 60 kilometers = 2 hours and 18 minutes
Run: 5 minutes per kilometer x 15 kilometers = 1 hour and 15 minutes

Total weekly training time = 4 hours and 33 minutes
Average daily workout time = 38 minutes per day

If you fit this example, you need to train an average of 38 minutes per day to be in tri-shape and to successfully complete a sprint distance triathlon. That's not very much time, so you will simply need to organize your priorities to fit in that 38-minute period each day. If you want to train only six days a week, that's fine, too. Your average daily workout time will still be only 46 minutes per day, if you want to take a day off during your week. (The specifics of this amount of training in the training program were discussed in Chapter 6.)

Here are the tables for determining your various training volumes based on the power of the distance. Start at the level that most closely resembles your last consistent week of training, and progress when the hunger gets

TRAINING SCHEDULES USING POWER OF THE DISTANCE				
Level 1: Novice (Train at this level for 2–4 weeks)				**Approximate Daily Time**
Power of 1:	1K swim	20K bike	5K run	14 min.
Level 2: Initiate (Train at this level for 4–8 weeks)				
Power of 2:	2K swim	40K bike	10K run	27 min.
Level 3: Experienced Beginner (Train at this level until you are ready to move to the intermediate stage)				
Power of 3:	3K swim	60K bike	15K run	38 min.
Level 4: Intermediate (Train at this level for 4–12 weeks)				
Power of 4:	4K swim	80K bike	20K run	53 min.
Level 5: Advanced				
Power of 5:	5K swim	100K bike	25K run	66 min.
Level 6: Competitor				
Power of 6:	6K swim	120K bike	30K run	80 min.
Level 7: Elite or Pro				
Power of 7:	7K swim	140K bike	35K run	1.5 hrs.
Power of 8:	8K swim	160K bike	40K run	1.75 hrs.
Power of 9:	9K swim	180K bike	45K run	2.0 hrs.
Level 10: Ironwoman				
Power of 10:	10K swim	200K bike	50K run	over 2 hrs.

46 min if 6 day PLAN

4.33 hrs total for 7 day period

stronger and the workouts seem easier. Your rate of progression is based as much upon subjective information as objective.

As you become more dedicated to tri-training and your fitness level increases, you will want to increase your weekly training levels to the power of four or five training systems. At this point, you are ready to consider racing longer than sprint distance races and have become an inspired triathlete.

"I am not going to quit on myself or do it for someone else."

TRAIN, DON'T EXERCISE—GET IGNITED

We are all competitors because we are all racers. Achieving your personal best in triathlon makes for good competition. You can compete against others (an old nemesis for instance), you can compete against the clock to see a time you've visualized, or you can compete to meet or beat your previous performance. Ultimately, it's about competition within you, with your conflicting priorities and life choices. Some say that training for high performance is mainly the domain of competitive athletes. But I feel if we examine competition more closely, there's likely a spark of competition that has been ignited in every one of us at every fitness level. So jump in, try some peak training, and go faster!

> ### An Ode to Training
>
> *If you want to race fast, train fast.*
> *If you want to race slow, train slow.*
> *If you want to race well, learn your heart zones.*
> *If you want to race smart, maximize your training.*
>
> *You may want it today.*
> *You probably will get it tomorrow.*
> *Systematically plan your training.*
> *Systematically train your plan.*
> *It can be yours.*
> *The winner is the one who has the most fun.*
> *—Sally Edwards*

In triathlon training, a little goes a long way. We look for every excuse to bring us back to our comfort level. You can get to a new height of fit and fast, though it will take time. Remember, you have annual, seasonal, macro, and weekly plans to work on. Plain old-fashioned, nothing-fancy discipline is a big part of a winning plan that gets you faster. By planning the workouts and working out according to plan, you are practicing what sports psychologists call "patterning." Patterning is repeating an action until it is so ingrained that your brain doesn't have to make a decision; it (and your heart) just follows a natural course, like brushing your teeth.

Your weakest sport may encourage a discipline problem. The clues are lackluster or missed workouts because of other commitments. Counter-attack with creativity. Invite a friend to participate, ride your bicycle to a bakery where friends can meet you (with a car complete with bike rack), swim in a different pool, or go to a fun run or race. Keep the days fresh with variety, and you will begin to enjoy your weak sport more and avoid it less.

A missed workout is difficult for many people to handle. The best solution to this problem is to go on to the next day; *do not* try to make up for the loss by adding those lost miles/meters/times to other days. Return to your plan. Injury is one of the prices you might pay for making a sudden jump in your training load.

Sure, there will be booby traps along the way. Even after you develop discipline and focus, outside influences will be eager to disrupt your plans. Booby traps are the inevitable obstacles in an active athlete's life. If you miss some workouts, and believe me, we all do, it's okay. By getting back on your plan and monitoring your workouts, you'll be able to include high-intensity training. You can train yourself to be more powerful by doing intervals and anaerobic training, and you will get faster. It will take time.

Your Individual Results

In addition to building discipline, you may also find it hard to focus on your true results. Your progress at this level of training might not seem as notice-able as in the previous stages. You are now starting to fine-tune a smooth triathlon machine. When someone moves from doing no activity to doing some activity, the benefits are obvious and significant. As you approach the limits of your fitness, improvement in performance, muscle development, and stamina, it won't appear to be in proportion to the amount of training you invested. Rather, at this level you are putting in an increasing amount of effort for smaller returns. Each percentage point of fitness and skill improvement costs more than the previous point. You must be kind and patient with yourself at this level because you may find your improvements hard to detect.

It is that last, hard-won 10 percent that makes a difference at the finish line, but discovery and experimentation will help you be able to say, "I did my best."

Getting Faster

One tool in every high-performance program is interval training. Intervals add variety both in your training load and your training response (adaptations) so you can most efficiently improve your fitness level. An "interval" consists of a period of high-intensity exercise followed by a period of rest, either total rest (complete stop) or active recovery (going slow). For a cyclist, active rest recovery means to shift down to a low gear and spin easy. For a swimmer, you'd continue to swim but use a different stroke, such as the breaststroke, for active recovery.

Here's an interval workout that's adaptable to any sport. Warm up at 50–60 percent of max HR for at least 10 minutes. Next, increase the intensity to 80 percent of max HR and hold for 1 minute before easing down to 60 percent of max HR for 2 minutes. Repeat this four times and then cool down at 50 percent of max HR. As this session becomes easier, add time to the work interval and keep the rest time as you transfer between a 1:2 to 2:1 to 2:2 ratio of work to rest.

Daily Intensity Training

How do triathletes train at high aerobic and anaerobic training volumes and continue each year to get faster, setting new records and pushing the outer boundaries of triathlon further and further?

Clearly, professionals train with high training volumes, some as high as 1,400 hours per year. They didn't start there, though; they trained up to that volume. They have reached their current fitness potentials by gradually developing and refining their biomechanical skills, studying strategy, developing personally, and maturing physically. There is one additional reason pros can train to such heights: cross-training.

The nature of triathlon offers the opportunity to alternate high-intensity training sessions on a daily basis. Accentuate the specific skill that is your intensity activity for the day. For example, one day you train hard (i.e., with high intensity) in swimming (not using your running or biking muscles), the next day hard in cycling (resting your swimming and running muscle groups), and the next day hard in running (resting your swimming and cycling muscle groups). In this way, you can train hard in one skill every day, but you will alternate your training in such a way that the sport-specific muscles of two systems always get at least one day of rest. Your cardiorespiratory system gains fitness while you are simultaneously resting alternate muscle groups. And remember to alternate among all three sports on different days, so that your conditioning will be balanced.

Anaerobic Threshold Ride

This is a strenuous bike ride and not for the faint of heart. After you are warmed up adequately, you are ready to begin a 20-minute steady-state heart rate. If you are trying to raise your anaerobic threshold (AT), you will be holding that heart rate or slightly higher. Depending on your fitness level, your AT could average anywhere between 70 percent and 95 percent of your max HR. Think of it as trying to hold the highest heart rate you can for 20 minutes. Rest and recover for 5 minutes, then repeat the 20-minute riding as hard as you can sustain. This workout is for only the fit and the fittest. It isn't easy because for most of us the ride is a zone 4 threshold ride. This is ideal training once a month to see if your average heart rate improves, that is, if it slowly goes up. The closer your anaerobic threshold heart rate is to your maximum heart rate, the fitter you are. The fitter you are, the faster you can go!

Overtraining and Injury

The flip side of getting faster is the possibility that you might overtrain. Overtraining is one of the most common causes of sports injury. Several good indicators in heart rate numbers and other data can keep you from overtraining. You also want to listen to your body. Loss of appetite, irritability, sleep disturbance, an elevated morning heart rate, lower than usual training heart rate, and repetitive colds and sniffles can be signs you may be overtraining.

In your quest to be faster and go farther, overtraining (and undertraining) are to be avoided rather than feared. Consistent logging of your workouts throughout the year can keep you feeling good about your workload. Triathlon logs such as the one I developed, *The Triathlon Log,* allow you to monitor and record and plan a reasonable workload quickly and efficiently. You can review your athletic diary and see how you've charted your way to success and possibly where you've overextended yourself.

When you are in good shape, you feel good about yourself all day. Following are ways to judge for yourself how hard your individualized heart zones training session should be today.

Delta Heart Training

Delta heart rate is an indicator of current health and stress condition of the individual. If the delta number varies by more than five beats per day or test, this is an indication that you should be aware of stress or other adverse conditions in your life. European athletes commonly perform this delta test and use the change in delta HR to determine daily training workload. American athletes tend to use high daily variation in resting heart rates as their indicator of overtraining. Either way, you'll want to monitor and record the following test:

Instructions:
1. Lie down in a comfortable horizontal position.
2. Relax completely for 2 minutes.
3. Look at your monitor at the end of 2 minutes. Remember this rate. This is your resting heart rate.
4. Stand up.
5. Watch your heart rate increase to a high point and then drop. Stay stationary for 2 minutes.
6. Enter these three numbers:
   Heart rate lying down: _____ bpm (B)
   Heart rate after standing for 2 minutes: _____ bpm (A)
   Calculate your delta heart rate: (A) minus (B) = _____

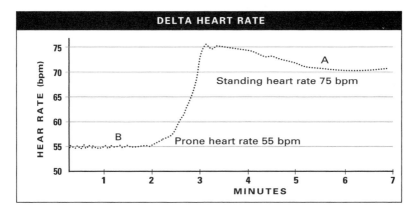

Available Time

If you think about it, you have one thing in common with a professional athlete: the same 24 hours in a day. The problem is, they have too much time to train and could possibly overtrain, whereas you may have too little time. You might try to compensate for too little time by cutting some important corners (sleep, meals with family) to get in your workouts. If a workday consists of 8 hours, this means you have three full 8-hour workdays in each 24-hour period. If you spend one 8-hour workday at an income-producing job, and you sleep another 8-hour workday, you still have one bonus workday left to use as you wish—for training and other activities.

Training for triathlons truly requires that you learn to deal with time. You will be asking yourself to juggle the time demands of training schedules, sleep requirements, professional work, your family, and, finally, your own personal growth, in a day that contains only 24 hours. You may often feel that you now waste time, thinking (usually without justification) that you simply are unable to accomplish as much as you would like to in one day.

If there's a consistently huge difference between the time you have and the demands you place on your time, you will crash and burn. Stay ignited, and find a new way to relate to time. Referees call time; prisoners serve time; musicians mark time; historians record time; slackers kill time; statisticians keep time; athletes race against time. The fact remains that we are all given the same amount of time. There are 24 hours in a day, 168 hours in a week. Use them fully—live every moment.

Distance

In order to finish a race distance, as a general rule, you need to train up to about 70 percent of the distances in any workout. For an international distance triathlon, the distances are 1-mile swim, 25-mile bike ride, and 6.2-mile run. So, to finish an international distance triathlon, on average, you want to be able to swim 30 minutes (0.7 of a mile), ride about 90 minutes (18–20 miles), and run 45 minutes (4–5 miles). You can most likely count on that extra 30 percent coming from race-day exhilaration and the joy of knowing that your long training is finally at a natural, expected conclusion. And in case the ultimate long-distance triathlon challenge is interesting to you (and I encourage you to imagine it), an Ironman race distance is 2.4-mile swim, 112-mile bike ride, and 26.2-mile (a marathon) run. Sprint triathlons (750-meter or 0.5-mile swim, 20-kilometer or 12-mile bike, 5-kilometer or 3-mile run) are no walk in the park, however, and most professional sprint triathletes train long distances to condition themselves as well.

Workload Increases

Workload is a concept that combines the amount (or the volume or quantity) and intensity (the quality) of stress applied in a specific training bout. For example, if you are swimming and the individual workout calls for 5 x 200 easy and 10 x 100 anaerobic (hard) intervals, the workload is 2,000 yards with 50 percent easy and 50 percent hard. If the next day you run 5 repeat miles at a fast 7 minutes per mile, with a 2-minute rest between each, your workload is 5 interval/hard miles at a 3.5 to 1 work-to-rest ratio. That's for 35 minutes running (7-minute miles times 5 miles) against 10 minutes rest (2-minute rests each times the 5-mile repeats), so the ratio is 35 minutes to 10 minutes, or 3.5 to 1. Here's the rule on workload: Increase either distance or intensity in a workout week but not both in the same week and never more than 10 percent per week at a time. To assess workload, you can look at the ratios or 10 percent in run miles, heart zones points, or total workout minutes, whichever works for you.

Double and Triple Workouts—Getting Faster

One way to increase training volume is to increase the number of individual workouts in one day. In the beginning, you'll want to be training 3–6 times weekly, with no more than one workout each day and at least one full day of total rest within each week. Later, after the lifestyle changes start to sink in, an aspiring triathlete adds to her training volume by increasing both training distance and the number of training sessions. You'll still want to take one day of rest per week, but you might choose to increase from six workouts per week to ten by adding multiple workouts to one or more days. Age groupers and professional athletes usually average between 1 1/2 and 2 1/2 workouts per day, adding up to a week that consists of 9–14 training sessions.

In determining which sports to combine on double-workout days, consider your daily schedule so that training fits into your home and professional lifestyle. Since running and cycling both require lower body stress, triathletes specifically train in both sports in a "brick" workout. This term is derived from the name of the person who first advocated using this type of training, but it also describes how your legs feel after you master this combination workout—hard as bricks!

Progressively increase from one double workout per week to several, eventually adding your first triple workout to your week's schedule. Start with six workouts per week and gradually add workouts until you reach your goal. Here is a sample training grid that shows how you can eventually include twelve workouts per week:

SAMPLE TRAINING GRID							
	Sun	Mon	Tue	Wed	Thu	Fri	Sat
Swim	OD	—	IN	—	EN	—	R
Bike	R	—	—	IN	—	EN	OD
Run	OD	—	EN	R	—	IN	—

OD refers to an "over-distance" workout. It's a lower-intensity (70 percent max HR), conversational pace lasting anywhere from 15 minutes to 1 hour depending on your fitness. Over-distance is similar to the long slow distance (LSD) workouts discussed in Chapter 5.

R stands for recovery. This is a run/walk session, a slow bike ride, or swim drills.

IN refers to intervals. A windtrainer is a great place for bike intervals. You'll want to approach the race pace at 80–90 percent of your max HR for short periods during this workout.

EN is short for endurance. This workout puts you at the top of zone 3, using 70–80 percent of your max HR. It's as long or short as you can endure without increasing your HR.

Adding triple-workout days requires planning, especially since few of us are full-time triathletes. Triple days are usually part of your day off from work or school, because they are time-demanding. Back-to-back triples (performing all three workouts with no rest between them) resemble a triathlon time trial and are recommended only if you want to train for the transition. Otherwise, it is best to rest between each workout on double- or triple-workout days to allow your metabolic reserves to rebuild and to enhance each individual workload session.

To get faster, work into each sport three workouts three times a week, or a total of nine workouts, very gradually. Spend time in your weakest sport. In general, look for a pattern of 20–25 percent swim, 40–50 percent bike, and 20–25 percent run when you are designing your weekly workouts, because this closely resembles the race effort.

When you have progressed to triple-workout days, you must intensely tune in to your body and its signals. There are side effects to overtraining, just as there are to undertraining, and you need to pay heed to potential problems from overuse or misuse of your body.

Periodization (Variability) Training

When I was training for the 1984 Olympic Marathon trials, after barely qualifying with a two-hour and fifty-minute finish at the Phoenix Marathon, I used a training cycle called hard/easy days. One day I would run hard, which always meant either short or long intervals, and the next day I would run easy or continuous easy, which was usually long-distance training.

A more advanced application of hard/easy training is using the heart zones training system that includes periodization, a system that varies the intensity and the amount (volume) of training within an individual macro/monthly cycle. Periodization, or variability, training is well suited to the body's cycles of exertion and recovery, and allows the body to spend time both resting and training hard, when that is what's necessary. The periods are groups of workouts that gradually improve fitness level (base) and increase sharpness for competition (peaks).

As an example, imagine one of your six training cycles (discussed in the previous chapter) is planned over an eight-week period. During that eight-week plan, you structure a period of three weeks that build (hard), with a fourth week that is easy (for recuperation), followed by a three-week period that builds to a new fitness level, which in turn is followed by a one-week recuperation period. This periodization is designed either to help you reach another branch on the training tree, or to prepare you for a peak of competition.

Variability Training of a Training Tree Branch

Periodization allows a progressive increase in the intensity and volume of the workload, resulting in quicker exercise adaptation. If, for example, you selected a four-week periodization cycle, you might use the first three weeks of the monthly/macro cycle for the body to adapt by gaining fitness; during the fourth week it adapts to the rest period by recuperating, so that it can accept greater workloads during the next four-week period of the macro cycle.

In periodization, training loads and intensities are increased progressively, so that the body adapts and improves instead of breaking down or weakening. However, not everyone adapts best to the same periodization pattern. Experiment here. Try alternating weeks in a 30-20-30-20 percent periodization, especially if you race every two weeks with the race falling on the easy 20 percent weeks. Shape the periodization cycle so that it fits your training and racing schedule. The heart zones training system (see Chapter 2 for details, but for example, 1 minute in zone 3 is three heart zone points— X minutes multiplied by zone number equals your points) easily allows for periodization in training by weekly changing points earned, such as weeks that accumulate 500 points, then 1,000 points, then 1,500 points.

Strength Training

Training with weights (also known as resistance training) is an effective way to build muscle. As women, we are in little danger of building bulk, but with regular strength training we can tone and strengthen, which enhances our performance. Since weight training builds muscle, which increases your metabolism, you'll burn more fat when you train. It is also a good way to keep your bones strong and dense, which will help prevent osteoporosis. Even using two-pound hand weights at home will help build strength. If you have never trained with weights, the best way to start is to find a trainer who can teach you how. Proper form is important to prevent injury, so it's good practice to have someone to watch your form and spot for you (help hold if the weight is too heavy).

If you don't have access to a gym for weight training, you can buy inexpensive rubber training tubes with handles for the same purpose. These come in various levels of stretch, so as you improve you can use a tube that doesn't stretch as much and therefore offers more resistance. Another advantage of tubes is that they're small and lightweight and thus good for travel.

Stretching

Stretching is a key activity for avoiding injury. Stretch every day. Stretch all the muscles in your legs and your lower back and neck with every run. With biking it's important to stretch your lower back, quads, and hamstrings, and with swimming you need to stretch your arms and shoulders. If you don't stretch on a daily basis, your muscles will get tight. This can pull on your joints and cause pain and injury. I cannot emphasize enough how important stretching is. It will make you feel better, you'll perform better, and you'll also make your muscles long and lean with enough stretching.

Rules and Guidelines for Heart Zones Training

As you progress through the heart zones training tree, there are a few standards you will want to follow. These guidelines will make an especially big difference as you climb onto the peaking and racing branches of your tree.

1. 24-HOUR RULE

If you are cross-training, you can do a zone 5 or upper zone 4 workout every 24 hours if it involves a different sport activity.

2. 48-HOUR RULE

After a red-line or upper zone 4 workout, you need to take a 48-hour break before you can train again in this specific sport activity. The reason is that the specific muscle recovery process requires 48 hours for replenishment.

3. 10 PERCENT RULE

A single day's red-line (zone 5) workout should not exceed 10–15 percent of the total training time for the week.

4. 25 PERCENT RULE

Total workout time in zones 4 and 5 should not exceed 25–35 percent of your total training time.

5. RATE, NOT PACE

It is more important to know your heart rate than your velocity or pace. That is, it is better to know at what percentage of your maximum heart rate you are training than to know your speed.

When I hear timers calling out my minute-per-mile pace as I run, I use their cue to remind me that I need to listen to my heart rate monitor and not to them. The primary reason not to use pace or bike speed or other external data cues is that it doesn't relate to other conditions such as temperature or altitude change.

What happens to your pace when the temperature increases fifteen degrees, when you hit the hills on the course, when there is shade, when you missed the aid station, or when your blood glucose levels drop? Your heart rate monitor will quantify your physiological responses to the various racing stresses in real time, whereas the best the race clock can do is give you a historical perspective. That time they call out is the elapsed time from your last mile, your after-the-fact pace. What about now and the next mile? I have been using my HRM for the past twenty years, and I am still surprised by the difference between what I perceive about my pace or rate and the HRM data. My recommendation is that you train using all systems: time, perceived exertion, and heart rate.

6. AT-ABOUT-AROUND

If the goal (and the true definition of cardiovascular fitness) is to raise your anaerobic threshold heart rate as close as possible to your max HR, then high-performance triathletes who have reached the speed branch on the training tree need to spend at least 25 percent of their weekly time at-about-around their anaerobic threshold heart rate. Remember, this is a moving heart rate number; as you get fitter, it moves toward your max HR, and one of the best ways to raise your anaerobic threshold is to train as close as possible to it.

7. HEART SPARING

Your upper heart rate limits are very stressful on every system in your body. Overtraining is frequently the result of spending too much time in the upper two zones. Blend the upper and lower zones and consciously calculate how much time you train in the upper zones so that you practice good heart-sparing training.

8. ZONES ARE PROGRESSIVE

Heart zones are positive and progressive stresses to the training system. As a result, the body learns to adapt to these stresses and improve. The three systems stressed are muscles, energy, and cardiovascular. By progressively increasing the intensity component, improvement occurs sequentially.

9. NARROW YOUR ZONES

The narrower you can shrink the zones, the more precise your training. Ultimately, the goal is to establish specific individual heart rates that are key training indexes to use in ultra-high-performance training. If you narrow the threshold zone from its big twenty-beat window down to a narrow five-beat window that includes your anaerobic threshold point, then train at-about-around that point, you've learned fine-tuned training.

10. THE 5-BEAT RULE

If your morning resting heart rate (before you get out of bed) is five beats above your normal average, drop your training for the day by at least one zone or take a complete rest day. An incrementally increased resting heart rate is an excellent indicator of overstressing your body's systems and is a warning sign or a wake-up signal to back off.

11. HIGHEST SUSTAINABLE HEART RATE

One of the secrets of racing with your heart rate monitor is to sustain the highest heart rate number that you can over the entire period of the event. Your highest sustainable heart rate is an individual heart rate number; for high-performance athletes, it's a number you pick out of your imagination or your dreams or aspirations, but in reality it is a heart rate number that you have trained at and know intimately because it is that borderline heart rate that could take you to either side: success or blowup. Train and know well your highest sustainable heart rate before the race. Time trial this heart rate number. For races longer than twenty minutes, it is probably below your anaerobic threshold, depending on environmental factors.

12. AS TRAINING INTENSITY INCREASES, TRAINING VOLUME DECREASES

Training intensity identifies the quality of exercise effort and is related inversely to volume. If you are training more time in the higher zones, then you need to decrease the quantity of training done during the specific workout session (training volume).

The Thrill of Achievement

You are the source of your performance. You can't blame others, circumstances, or conditions. Some people may obstruct you, and some may help you enthusiastically, but you are the one who either puts them off or invites them aboard. You determine your own success and your own failure. You are now in the best overall condition of your life.

A GUIDE TO DIAGNOSING TRAINING

Here's a chart that demonstrates how you might use your HR data to make subtle changes in your exercise workload throughout your planning cycles.

Resting/Delta HR	Training HR	Speed	Description
Normal	Normal	Normal	Everything is fine. Train normally.
Normal	↑	↓	Commonly occurs during base training. Indicates you are training too hard.
Normal	↓	↑	This commonly occurs after a high-intensity interval workout. Take a low zone recovery workout or take the day off.
↑	↑	↓	Fatigue state. Warning: Immunity system might be compromised.
Normal	↑	Normal	Training speed may even be dropping. Symptomatic of dehydration.
Normal	↑	↓	Indicates tiredness.
Normal	Normal	↓	Indicates tiredness or "dead legs."
↑	Normal	Normal	Indicative of minor stress, worry, mental anxiety, or concern.
Normal	↓	↓	Both training heart rate and speed drop, which indicates a chronic, seriously fatigue condition.
↑	↓	Normal	Unable to maintain training HR; symptomatic of overtraining.

↑ means higher HR numbers than normal.

↓ means lower HR number than normal.

Normal means consistent or similar heart rate numbers.

It hasn't been easy. It hasn't happened quickly. It hasn't been without sacrifice. Rarely are the accomplishments that we strive for achieved without giving. It hasn't been without direction, for you have modeled yourself in pursuit of goals and good habits. It hasn't been without knowledge, for with the help of heart rate monitor training principles, you can grow toward achieving your full potential.

There are times when you are so focused on what you have set for yourself as achievement that once that level is obtained, you the athlete might lose perspective. The triathlon event is not everything in life, but it can be life changing. Being reminded of what you have already achieved by participating in a mentoring capacity creates a healthy appreciation for your abilities. Through a triathlon community composed of many performance levels, such as created by the Danskin Mentor-Mentee program, a dose of reality creates a balanced and compassionate look at yourself and other triathletes.

We can all be victors in the challenges we set for ourselves, but to be superwinners, you must accept the additional challenge of lending your experience and knowledge to others. When the race is over, life still goes on, and the next day brings fresh opportunities. Lending your voice and helping build a network of women triathletes in the Danskin Mentor-Mentee Program will enable you to build relationships, share experiences, and continually be reignited in your triathlon quest. Why not volunteer by going to www.mentor-mentee.org?

The human being is one of the most awesome athletic machines to ever walk the planet. When we thrill to an event like the Olympics, we're not responding to whose training regime was the best or which country had the best nutritionist. Instead we resonate and respond to people who grasp a small part of that potential in each one of us and reach out. It is the reach to others that is important. I have been lucky enough to stand at the starting lines with great athletes, and I've been privileged to make whatever small marks I've made. But what I have come to learn is that the reach is more important than the grasp.

The winner is the one who has the most fun.

RACING

Getting yourself to the finish line of a triathlon may be one of your "large goals." If so, I'd like to help you get there. If not, I'd like to encourage you to reconsider. Participating in a triathlon can be as large or as small a step as you make it. You can aim toward competing in an Ironman (as an Ironwoman), or simply sign up for your next local "Tri for Fun," which is usually a brief, self-competitive event. In any case, be reasonable with yourself. Success at racing—just doing a triathlon—always involves honestly evaluating your strengths and weaknesses, as well as setting realistic goals.

You'll want to break the event into five parts—three separate sporting events connected by two transitions. Think of each event as having an individual starting and finish line (they do). Then, link three great races together with two fast and efficient transitions.

Prevent failure by preparing well: Be meticulous with your equipment, hydrate (drink lots of liquids) before the race, and eat and sleep well during the days and nights before.

Warm up your mind before the race, as well as your body. Think through the whole race day so thoroughly that you know the race as well as if you had already completed it. This will help eliminate the pre-race jitters and get you into a performance mind-set.

Acknowledge that there will be pain. Exhaustion and discomfort are part of the entry fee that's paid to reach the finish line, so go ahead and pay the price, but only up to a point. When you near the point where pain is verging on bodily overextension or breakdown, back off. It's better to finish upright than to practice the "triathloid crawl."

Tap into and refine the source of your energy—the mind/body union. Listen intently to both the sounds of your mind's chatter and the feelings of your heart and lung exertion. Fine-tune both to maximize your efficiency, and relax into the experience as best as you can.

Grow from the triathlon experience. If you have a disaster, a broken bike, a slow swim, or a person who looks less fit who passes you, use those experiences for what they were meant to be: lessons. Link the lessons together, and you will watch your performance grow.

Last, remember to live it up. Doing a triathlon is like a big party—the actual event may be the main attraction, but the sideshow is almost as much fun. Meet new people, share stories, eat, drink, and be the merriest of them all—you will deserve it.

The Heart of the Matter: Transitions

The heart of triathlons is the transition between the events: T1, the swim-to-bike, and T2, the bike-to-run. If you've reached the point in your training where you've developed sufficient skill and endurance in each of the three sports skills to consider entering a race, knowing how to transition efficiently will be the last piece in your winning puzzle.

Add proper transition preparation to your training program. Take a swim and transition onto a bike ride, and, likewise, ride and transition onto a run. Mental preparation is important, so visualize yourself transitioning through each step in an orderly fashion, and it will become a familiar experience.

At the Danskin Triathlon Series New York race, I watched a woman walk up the chute to the bike transition area after the swim, the last person to finish out of 400-plus women. I don't know her name—she was one of thousands of women immersed in their first triathlon on that day. She met two of her supporters there who had managed to get into the transition area to help her, and she said to them, "I can't believe I did it." It was one of the happiest moments of her life. She hadn't known if she could swim that far, in open water, in a strange lake, with thousands of other triathletic women, but she did it. "I have never been so scared in my whole life," she confided. Now that the swim leg was completed, she wasn't worried about the 20K bike and the 5K run.

There was no urgency in her actions. She sat down and ate a sandwich, chatted with her friends about the joy and thrill of her accomplishments, and finally left the swim-to-bike transition area about ten minutes later.

Meanwhile, Fernanda Keller, the Danskin-sponsored pro triathlete, transitioned in forty-five seconds. She was totally focused on time, not social chatting, because she needed to catch Lisa Laiti, who had been first out of the transition area. Lisa crashed on her bike soon after, though, and didn't finish the race. But the last-place woman swimmer did finish — she may not have tried to catch anyone on the bike leg, and she probably walked rather than ran the 5K run. But she did it — she finished.

How to Get Organized for Transitions

You'll find it helps to plan your transitions in advance. Prepare a list of all of the equipment you may need and save it for future reference. Practice transitions to figure out what works for you. Here's my complete list, but since everyone is different, keep a list that fits you:

Swim	Bike	Run
Swimsuit	Helmet	Running shoes
Goggles	Bike	Visor
Gear bag	Bike tools	Race number
Swim cap	Sunglasses or	
Wrist watch	eye protectors	*Optional:*
or HRM	Shoes/cleats	Socks
	Water bottles	Running shorts
	Bike pump	Heart rate monitor
Optional:	Bike number	Lace locks
Wetsuit		
Goggle defogger		
Race belt	*Optional:*	**Transition Gear**
Trisuit	Bike computer	Towel
Safety pins	Air cannisters	Food and drink
Bike shorts	Cold-weather	Camera
Food	apparel	Post-race clothes
Sunscreen		Plastic bag for rain
Cycling gloves		
Fanny pack		
Vaseline		

Putting Together the Pieces: Race-Day Preparation

Two nights before the race, get a good night's sleep. This is the most important night, since you might be too nervous or excited the night before the race to sleep well.

The night before the race, set out all your gear and make sure you have everything you need for the race. Check that your swimsuit, cap, and goggles are there. Make sure your bike helmet, gloves if you plan to wear them, sunglasses or clear eye protection, and bike shoes are in your race bag. Don't forget your race number and running shoes. Put the bike number on the bike, and clip your number onto your race belt or pin it to the shirt you'll wear for the run. Put your full water bottles in the bag or on the bike, have an energy bar or other quick food in your bag in case you need it, and bring along some clothes to wear after the race. Mentally walk yourself through the entire race, and see if you've forgotten anything. Then you'll be ready to go in the morning, without worrying about your equipment.

Transition Setup

The morning of the race, arrive an hour early so that you can test your gear, go through your body marking (a number will be written on your arms and legs with felt pens), take care of calls from nature, relax, and stretch.

Shoelace locks can save you 15–30 seconds in transition.

In the bike transition area, numbered racks will be set up that will correspond with the entrants' race numbers. Find yours. Once there, organize your bike gear. Lay down a towel and place on it your bike shoes or cleats (unless you have them attached to your clipless pedals), your shirt, and race belt (with your race number attached to either). Then hang your helmet and sunglasses on your bike frame, and check that your water bottles are full.

Next, give your bike a final inspection. Check the tire pressure and brakes. Then test ride the bike and put it in the gear you want to use when you first start out of the area. Make sure you have everything you need: tire repair tools and a tube, a frame pump or air canisters, and your cyclometer (if you have one), cleared and set. Finally, rack your bike, and stop and get your bearings. Pick a nearby landmark and use it as a guidepost for locating your bike after the swim. You might be a little disoriented when you get out of the water, so you need to be able to find your bike without too much effort.

Next, set up your transition area for the run. Set out the gear in the order that you are going to put it on—socks (optional), running shoes, a visor or hat (optional), and any personal items such as sunscreen. You're now done, unless the transition areas are in two different locations. In that case, set each up with its own towels and gear arrangements.

Walk over to the finish of the swim and look at the setup. Memorize what the exit looks like, including its terrain and footing, then look back at your bike and visualize how you will walk/run to get to your bike at the end of the swim (many triathletes forget where they have racked their bikes and waste time searching, since they didn't set a guidepost). Don't neglect to walk over to the start of the swim and select markers, such as buildings or trees, that you can use as sighting points during the swim, because it's almost impossible to swim in a straight line. Finally, walk over to the exit of the bike course as well, so that you are familiar with the exit and entry setup.

The Swim

The announcer will call you to the starting line. In most triathlons, you will begin the race in "waves." Waves are groups of individuals in the same age division who start separately, with delays usually of 2–5 minutes between each wave. Stand with the individuals who are marked with the same age division number as you; usually, everyone in the age group is wearing the same color cap.

Triathletes walking their bikes out of T1 to start the bike leg.

As the starting signal sounds for your wave, enter the water with measured caution. After a few strokes, stop if you want and take a few extra breaths. After you round the first buoy, take the time to get your bearings, breaststroke for a few yards, and remember to breathe.

As you round the last buoy and head back toward the shore, do a mental body check—survey your body and scan your energy level. Go ahead and swim as close to the finish as you can before you stand.

T1: Swim-to-Bike Transition

This transition starts about 100 yards from the finish of the swim, because it's then that you'll begin to visualize the finish line. As you reach the shore and put your feet down, you might feel dizzy—most of us do. Your equilibrium may be thrown off as you come from a prone to an upright position, but you'll regain it quickly. There may be volunteers in the water to help you; listen to their instructions, and take care to drink at the aid station.

In a controlled fashion, walk or run through the flagged area that has been constructed for a finishing chute and find your bike rack. If you are wearing a wetsuit, strip it off. Slip on your bike shoes or cleats, your shirt and shorts if you plan to wear them, your sunglasses, and your helmet (it must be buckled). Then take your bike off the rack, start your bike monitor or heart rate monitor, and either ride or walk the bike out of the transition area, whichever is required. The less time you spend in transition, the faster your finishing time.

Some of you may decide to change your clothes for each of the three events. I don't recommend it. To avoid the time-consuming process of clothes changing, I recommend that you swim in a Lycra suit or sports bra and Lycra fitness shorts, then slip on a pair of cycling or fitness shorts and leave them on for the run. You can wear a singlet or shirt for the run as well, but don't wear it on the bike unless it is cold, because the shirt will create greater wind resistance.

Enjoy the ride.

The Bike

I love the start of the bicycle leg. I am fresh, happy, and excited. What I need to do at that point is relax and ride according to my pre-race strategy—first, at a set speed, not at the pace that my heart is going, then later at a set heart rate, not pace.

As you start, remind yourself not to draft (since most triathlons don't allow it and you can be disqualified if you do), and remember to talk to riders as you approach them and shout out that you are passing. Always pass to the left, but don't ever cross the centerline of the road.

You should start drinking almost immediately from your water bottle, and if the bike portion is over 25 miles, you may need to eat during the ride as well.

As you near the second transition, remember to go slowly through the chicane (the traffic cones that are set up to slow you down as you ride into or out of a transition area), and get off and walk your bike in the transition area, because runners will be exiting down the corridors between the bike racks.

T2: Bike-to-Run Transition

Again, the transition starts before the finish of the bike, when you start to prepare mentally for the run. Drink as much fluid as you possibly can at this point, so that you are hydrated for the run start.

Once into the transition area, find the place that is assigned for your bike and rack it. Unbuckle your helmet after you get off the bike. Slip off your bike shoes, slide on your running shoes, put on a visor, add a shirt if you want one, put on your race number, and take off.

"I feel I have wings and I love the view from up here."

The Run

Immediately you will feel an entirely new sensation in your legs, what triathletes call "the grip." The changeover from using cycling muscles (those in the front of the thigh—the quadriceps) to running muscles (those located in the back of the thigh—the hamstrings) results in an incredible tightening. You will notice that you can't extend your legs as far as you would like and that your stride frequency (turnover rate) is impaired. It usually takes several hundred yards or as much as a couple of miles before your legs recover from the triathlon grip, but eventually you'll settle in to your chosen pace.

Other runners will pass you, just as swimmers and cyclists may have. You will pass other runners as well. Those with strong backgrounds in all three parts of the race rarely get passed. Balance is the solution to winning in this sport.

As you approach the final finish line, look up—there will be a finish clock with the time. It's guaranteed to display the wrong time, because it will be measuring the time from the first wave, and you are probably in one of the later ones. Remember the time, though, so that you can subtract your wave handicap when you are thinking more clearly. Better still, look at your wristwatch and rely on your own timing.

Finally, throw your shoulders back, hold your head up, and run across the finish line with a huge smile spreading across your face—you are a triathlete.

The most vivid highlights of my athletic career have occurred at the finish line of races. Running toward the finish banner, with the spectators applauding, the announcer saying my name over the loudspeaker, and looking up at a finish clock that reads the numbers that match my goal, is pure exhilaration. I have one overriding thought that always hits me at that moment. I think that if I had just known how good the finish-line experience would be, I would have trained more.

Francine Rosner, Cathy Anerson-Meyers, and Judy Payne, training and racing partners living the triathlon lifestyle.

TEN

THE WELLNESS CONTINUUM

I have often said that being "healthy" is a wellness continuum that flows from health to fit to performance. Health is mainly defined as the absence of injury and disease. Fitness takes you a step past health, and is the ability to perform physically. You can be relatively healthy while not fit, but you cannot be fit and not healthy. Good health is a prerequisite for fitness. Health combined with fitness takes you to wellness.

In the wellness balancing act, physical movement is one of the key forces. Training in heart zones by using a heart rate monitor is one of the most effective ways to connect your mind, emotions, and muscles together, which can lead you into the wellness continuum. When you reach this point, you have a credible chance of discovering the road in life that leads to your balance and wellness. It's your choice if you want to follow it.

First, let's look at the physical side of the heart and the use of heart rate technology. In both of my books *Heart Zone Training* and *The Heart Rate Monitor Guidebook to Heart Zone Training,* I discuss using a monitor as a fat-burning device for exercise to shed a few pounds of body fat. In it, I quote a report stating that obesity-related conditions cost an estimated 500,000 lives in the United States in 2001. For years, it was thought that people were dying from degenerative and other diseases in large part because of the effects of obesity. However, the latest research shows that we may have looked at the wrong health variable. Researchers have been studying fatness and not fitness, especially heart fitness. In fact, it appears that it's probably the lack of cardiovascular exercise, not the increase in fat, that seems to be taking so many lives.

According to Dr. Jody Wilkinson, medical director of the Cooper Institute for Aerobic Research in Dallas, Texas, "In fact, our habits have more to do with our mortality and what diseases we get than our body size does." She was quoting the 1996 report from her institute that showed thin people with poor physical fitness were more likely to die prematurely than overweight people who exercise regularly. The key and independent variable is exercise. Unfortunately, most exercise and nutrition specialists have focused on body fat, size, and shape than on lifestyle habits. Fat people can be fit, and fit people can be fat.

Common Discomforts

Several minor discomforts are associated with any exercise program. The thing to remember about all of them is that they are your body's way of letting you know that something is slightly out of balance. Toughing it out and ignoring pain is not a wise move, because willful ignorance can turn a minor problem into a major one.

Side Aches

Side aches, or "stitches," generally seem to be caused by overexertion. The exact cause of side aches is unknown, but it is suspected that gas caught in the upper intestine might be a frequent culprit. There are a few tricks that sometimes work to stop the pain:
- Put pressure from your fingers directly on the place that hurts.
- Massage the general area with your whole hand.
- Straighten your back and stretch tall.
- Relax your breathing and slow down the number of breaths you are taking per minute.
- Lean forward, bending at the waist.

Post-workout Nausea

Variously, this can be caused from eating too much just before a workout, or from not eating enough, so that your body doesn't have enough easily accessible calories with which to work. Nausea can also be caused by dehydration. Experiment with your drinking and eating patterns and see what helps.

Blisters

Blisters can be caused by shoes and/or socks that don't fit well, that have tight spots, or that are wet. Small blisters can be covered with medicated cream and a bandage. Large blisters should be drained with a sterilized needle, then treated with medicated cream and a covering. Pay attention to them because they can get infected.

Muscle Cramps

What feels like painful knots are actually involuntary contractions of the muscle. It is not known what causes them—it could be a lack of sodium, potassium, calcium, or a vitamin complex. To help get rid of the pain, stretch the joint, massage the area, and walk it off by gently moving the muscle. Then, evaluate your diet, and if cramps happen frequently, change your drinking and eating habits and see if that helps.

Injuries

Triathlon can be a dangerous sport. Once after a bike wreck I was being treated for lacerations and abrasions in the medical tent. My friend and pro triathlete Scott Molina was nearby, and I overheard him in a moment of utter exasperation releasing a few choice expletives regarding the bike leg of the event. The bike course was on the streets of the city, through major inter-sections that were closed to traffic. He had been in the lead, spinning through the streets at high speed, trusting that the course marshals had stopped all vehicles. However, just as Molina entered one intersection, a fire truck also sped through, responding to an emergency. The two missed by an inch.

It rattled him for a long time.

Tri-training can help you avoid many of the overuse injuries that plague single-sport specialists, because you alternate muscle groups in your workouts. On the other hand, triathletes also have to be wary of three times as many injuries as do single-sport athletes—we can get swimmer's shoulder, cyclist's knees, and runner's feet.

The most common injuries are the result of overuse and are generally of one of two types: stress fractures or inflammation (of the tendons, ligaments, bursas, cartilage, connective tissues, or nerve tissues).

All overuse injuries share the same common causes: repeated stress on a given structure that overwhelms its capacity to respond and repair itself. Or, quite simply, this can be caused by repetitive trauma from training errors.

Among runners, the most common cause of problems is excessive mileage, or the overtraining syndrome. Other causes are also in the too much or too soon categories:

- Too fast an increase in the distances in your training schedule
- Too much of an increase in resistance training, such as climbing hills
- Too much interval training, too soon
- Too many or too intense bounding or jumping exercises
- Too much time spent running on hard surfaces

Other injuries are caused by training errors, such as training in the wrong shoes, inadequate stretching/warming up, lack of adequate flexibility and/or strength, imbalanced muscle development, and uncompensated leg-length differences.

Injuries are common in both sexes and have been found to be more sport-specific than sex-specific. There are some indications that women may have a higher overall incidence of injury, but the injury patterns are the same. Women do appear to have a higher incidence of shin splints and stress fractures, but they also seem to have a lower incidence of certain types of tendinitis.

When I competed in the 1984 U.S. Olympic Marathon trials, my competition and I were surveyed, and researchers found that a high number (44 percent) of the 210 women reported that they had suffered from a musculoskeletal problem that they considered significant. Of those who qualified for the trials, 10 percent were unable to compete because they were injured at the time of the race.

Are women more at risk of overuse injuries than men?

It appears that there is a higher rate of injury among female athletes, but that it is predominantly caused by their lower initial levels of fitness. As women become more active and competitive, their rates of injury approach those of men.

Most people believe that women suffer from more knee problems than do men because of the wider female pelvis and greater joint flexibility. In fact, knee pain among runners is the most common injury for both sexes, occurring in 24 percent of the men and 27 percent of the women runners, which is not a significant difference.

It appears that women suffer from more stress fractures overall than do men, but some specific stress fractures may occur less often in women. Studies indicate that stress fractures of the iliac crest (the bone you feel when you put your hands on your hips) and the tarsal navicular (one of the bones in the middle and inside of the foot) are more predominant among men. Again, the increased rate of stress fractures, similar to other overuse injuries, is likely to be related to the initial lack of proper conditioning.

Another orthopedic stress trauma is swimmer's shoulder (pain from repeated trauma to the head of the upper arm bone). The incidence is higher among women (reported by 68 percent, versus 50 percent of men).

The most common problem for swimmers is ear infection, which is not gender-dependent. Ear infections are caused by exposure of the tissues in the ear canal to prolonged irritation. The best treatment is prevention—wearing earplugs and thoroughly drying the ears (there are chemicals that can do this). Once symptoms are present, you must decrease the inflammation and simultaneously treat the infection.

Treatment

For overuse injuries, rest is the best treatment. However, if your condition is serious, then casting, crutches, anti-inflammatory drugs, or physical therapy may be required. For nonserious injuries, it's permissible to treat it yourself first by using ice, compression, and elevation of the injured part.

Diagnose the pain, because you can't keep the problem from recurring if you don't know its cause. Every overuse injury is caused by a force on a tissue that is greater than the tissue's basic strength, and every injury-causing force can be traced to one of the following causes:

1. Training errors that do not allow for adequate recovery
2. Tissues that are weak and susceptible to injury
3. Biomechanical weaknesses that put excessive stress on certain parts of your body

When you know what caused it, you can begin to fix it.

Rehabilitation, using flexibility, strengthening, and aerobic/anaerobic conditioning, is the key to returning to your training program. If you are injured, cross-train in a different skill that doesn't hurt, until the pain disappears. If you continue to train with pain, you only exacerbate the problem and delay healing.

Upper Respiratory or Short-Term Illness

It's a tough call whether to exercise when you are sick. But it's better to be safe than sorry, so it's generally not a bad idea to take a few days off when your immune system is impaired by illness. If you must continue to train when you are ill, do so at a reduced amount and intensity.

For a cold, if you can take a few days off, do so. There is no proof that complete bed rest cures virus colds any faster, nor is there any proof that training extends the duration of a cold, but do take it easy.

If you have a fever, don't work out. Your heart is already working double time by maintaining metabolic function as well as pumping blood to the skin's surface in order to reduce the heat from the fever. Don't add a third load on your system.

Gynecological Concerns

The past two decades have brought hundreds of thousands of women into the world of exercise and athletic training. The medical experts have given them the green light—regular exercise can only improve the quality of women's lives.

Here are some of the conditions that can affect any woman, athletic or not, and the facts that relate to these conditions as they pertain to training.

Vaginitis

Training itself does not cause vaginitis, nor does it cure it. However, wearing nonbreathable training apparel can cause a moister than normal vaginal environment, which can encourage the overgrowth of yeast, the major cause of vaginitis (one of the common forms is known as a "yeast infection"). If you have a recurring problem with vaginitis (or even if you don't), it would be a good idea to wear training apparel made of breathable fabrics, such as cotton or rayon blends. In any case, if you notice the onset of vaginitis (the common symptoms are discharge, itching, odor, and discomfort), consult your gynecologist, who will treat it with appropriate medication.

Stress Urinary Incontinence

This is a condition of involuntary urine leakage, which occurs when there is an increase in abdominal pressure such as from jumping, running, or straining. It is not directly caused by sports activities and is usually found in women who have given birth several times. Training can cause an increase in abdominal pressure and, as a result, involuntary leakage symptoms, but exercise does not worsen a condition that is already present. Consult a urologist to determine the cause. To aid with the problem, empty your bladder before you train, follow specific exercises that can strengthen the muscles involved, and wear a minipad. Don't let this problem stop you from training.

Contraception
It's your call. Your decision on which type of contraceptive agent to use is not affected by the fact that you train. The decision is based solely on your choice of a safe and effective way of preventing conception.

Menstrual Irregularity
Any woman who has irregular menstrual cycles should consult a gynecologist to determine the cause. Irregular periods (amenorrhea) are indeed more common among athletically active women than sedentary women, but it is not known why. Athletic amenorrhea is a condition of menstrual irregularity caused by exercise. Amenorrhea may be caused by the physical stress of training, the emotional stress of competition, hormonal changes, possible loss of body weight due to increased physical activity, or a change in eating patterns. However, recent studies indicate that athletic amenorrhea may be primarily caused by eating disorders, not exercise, so don't stop training, and don't stop eating.

If you experience frequent, prolonged, heavy, or unexpected menstrual periods and there are no associated gynecological problems, it is not recommended that you try to manipulate your periods using hormones. Menstruation is an inconvenience, but it's just one of the things you deal with as a woman.

In athletic ammenorheic women, normal periods usually resume once training is reduced. Likewise, fertility is restored to normal upon resumption of a normal menstrual cycle.

Menstrual Cramps
For women who suffer from menstrual discomfort or pain, exercise has been shown to help alleviate symptoms. These strong and intermittent lower abdominal pains do not preclude you from working out. It's perfectly safe

to exercise at all times during the month. If menstrual cramps are frequently or regularly severe or debilitating, consult your gynecologist and try to keep training.

Pregnancy

One of your greatest athletic achievements may be getting fit before becoming pregnant and staying fit during pregnancy. If it isn't your greatest athletic achievement, it can still be one of your life's high times.

Even though physical conditioning is certainly good for pregnant women, there are certain precautions that must be followed. Training vigorously can result in excessive heat (hyperthermia), lowered oxygen supply that could reduce that of the fetus, inadequate blood flow, or abdominal traumas.

A program of general conditioning is desirable for moms-to-be; your pregnancy, labor, and delivery will all likely be easier for your efforts. However, always check with your obstetrician before starting or continuing a vigorous conditioning program. If you weren't training before you became pregnant, you shouldn't start on a program any more strenuous than walking. Weight training, stretching, and calisthenics are good conditioning activities for pregnant women.

Other Concerns
Anemia

A common affliction of female athletes, anemia is a disease characterized by an abnormally low number of red blood cells (RBC). It is usually caused by the loss of iron that occurs in menstruation, or by not eating sufficient iron-rich foods. Sometimes heavy training can cause a loss of iron through the intestines and in your stools. Athletic anemia is a condition of low RBC count, which is due to an increase in the volume of blood without a corresponding increase in the number of cells. This is not true anemia, but when you are training, your blood volume may increase by as much as 10 percent faster than your RBC concentration.

For whichever cause, one out of every four women in America is iron-deficient, and one out of twenty is anemic. To be iron-deficient means that your iron reserves (iron that is stored in your liver, spleen, bone marrow, and other tissues) are low. Once your iron stores are depleted, you become anemic. If you think you are anemic, check with your doctor. Self-medicating with large doses of iron can lead to problems with other nutrients.

Cancer and Exercise

Facing a diagnosis of cancer can evoke many responses, including fear, anger, depression, confusion, and hopelessness. Many cancer patients search for ways to take an active role in their treatment and recovery. One way a cancer patient can regain some sense of control in the direction of her health is through daily exercise. Individuals who have exercised regularly prior to cancer treatment have a higher tolerance to cancer treatment and recover more quickly. Breast surgeon Paula Oliver of the Capitol Surgeons Group in Austin, Texas, has found that "the stronger a patient is at the point of diagnosis, the better chance they have of tolerating the most effective treatment." Lisa Talbott, M.P.H. and co-founder of Team Survivor, believes that exercising throughout treatment keeps a patient's energy level up and, more important, hastens post-surgery and treatment recovery time.

For more information, see Appendix A.

Varicose Veins

The enlarged veins that appear near the skin's surface are not caused by exercise but by malfunctioning blood vessel valves. Exercise not only helps relieve the pain from varicose veins but also can help treat the condition. Do not confuse athletic veins with varicose veins. Some athletes have large veins because of their bodies' need to carry larger amounts of blood to the skin's surface for its thermoregulatory (cooling) effects.

Safety

Women are prime targets for physical abuse in any of its forms. Your responsibility (and it's unfortunate that you have to do this) is to reduce the opportunity for being a target.

Here are fifteen rules of safety for all triathletic women. Think about each one as you read them and ask yourself, "Do I do that?" Then, add these safety rules as key ingredients in your training regimen. Follow all fifteen—they are so important that you should think of them as laws, not rules.

1. **Beware of ruts.** It may seem logical to always run or ride at the same time of day, on the same course, in the same way, but don't. Assailants will often plan their attack around such habits, so vary your patterns and never allow them that opportunity.

A typical starting-line scene as women wait for their wave to start.

2. Never travel alone. Train with a partner. You are safest when someone else is with you. I once had an accident—I tripped while running alone and broke my ankle. The damage from walking home and dragging my bad foot caused months of delay in my recovery and left me an easy target.

3. Stay alert. Never trust that you are perfectly safe, because you aren't. Never block your senses while out training, such as by wearing headphones. It's vital that you are able to see and hear what is going on around you.

4. Beware of the night. Wear reflective gear whenever the lighting is insufficient: nights, early mornings, in fog or inclement weather. Purchase reflective patches and stick them on your shoes, your hat, everywhere, and always try to train in well-lit areas.

5. Practice prevention. Always be prepared for the worst-case scenario. Carry change or a cell phone to make a telephone call, have identification on you when you are out on the roads, and tell someone where you are going before you leave. An ounce of prevention may save your life.

6. Be aware that trouble can come anytime, from anybody. Attacks can happen at any time of day and by anyone. There is no average profile of an assailant—the only common denominator is that they are always male. And just because a stranger is dressed in a three-piece suit doesn't mean he isn't a rapist; rapists are getting more sophisticated.

7. Know your turf. Become familiar with the area in which you swim, bike, and run, and get to know some of the folks along the way. Know where there are police call boxes or telephones, and recognize where there is dense foliage or places for attackers to hide.

8. Have a plan. Make a decision about what you will do in different circumstances. For example, if someone enters your safety zone, that personal space that strangers may not violate, move away quickly.

9. Don't assume anything. Just because you have ridden a certain course for years without mishap doesn't mean it will be safe tomorrow. A local resident might have just adopted a stray dog that likes to attack cyclists.

10. Use anger. Anger may be your best weapon, because it can intimidate, buy you precious time, and make a potential attacker have second thoughts. You may even have to use profanity in your anger, and I believe that God will forgive you if you have to curse to stay alive.

11. Use something. Carry a whistle, a can of mace, or car keys—something so that if you have to fight, you have more than your hands and feet for weapons.

12. Don't talk with or stop for strangers. It is a rule you learned as a child but may have dismissed as an adult: Don't strike up a conversation unless you know the other person. If you are verbally harassed, ignore the individual involved. If you're being followed, stopping and staring at the person will let him know that you are not unaware and he is not unseen.

13. Be smart. Never wear expensive jewelry or watches when you train—it's amazing what people will do to take them from you. The less you have, the less likely you'll become a target.

14. If he is armed, you are supposed to give it to him. If it's a material item, by all means give it to an armed robber. If someone tries to rape you, I don't have a best solution. When I was in Vietnam during the war, an American GI attempted to rape one of my fellow Red Cross members who was sleeping in the quarters several doors away. She feigned an epileptic attack, and he left.

15. Turn an attacker in. If you are attacked, memorize everything—his face, size, clothes, anything unusual. Call the police as soon as possible, and do everything you can to help the police capture and prosecute him.

Physical violation is a form of terrorism that you may experience in your lifetime—eight out of every ten women do. Within a thousandth of a second, you will have to respond and make the right decision or pay a huge price. Some attackers are discouraged by anger, but flight might be more effective than fighting with others. In any case, the best cure for this particular illness, violence, is prevention. So be smart (see rule 13), and play by these rules of safety.

Moments after crossing the finish line of the 1998 Ironman Triathlon in Kona, Hawaii, Sally Edwards takes joy in her sixteenth time to finish in the last twenty years of racing in this, the world championships.

MATTERS OF THE
HEAD AND HEART

"If you, Sally, can run a hundred miles, finish sixteen Ironmans, qualify for the Olympic Marathon trials, complete the Eco-Challenge, win the women's team division in the bicycle event Race Across America, run a business, write over a dozen books, and stand up in front of an audience of a thousand and speak, then I can start a training program." I've heard this in various forms over the years, and I always respond by asking "What do you want to train for?"

Invariably the answer is "I want to train in order to change my life." Great. All things change when we do.

At the Danskin Triathlon, women who take those first few difficult steps, working toward making that difference in their lives, surround me. It isn't going to be easy at first, but you can do it.

Training For Enjoyment

Triathletes have been branded as pain-seeking athletes—the toughest of them all. I am always amazed when people ask me the "who" question, because when I answer that "I am a triathlete," a look of reverence appears. That didn't occur when I used to say I was an ultra-marathoner who won hundred-mile races in my pre-triathlon athletic era.

It's a myth that triathletes eat nails and only know how to talk to a bike, their running sneaks, or themselves as they float, coast, and shuffle. We are really simple folks. We train because we have fun at it, certainly not for the money or the fame, and usually not because of our egos. When I tell people that I have fun when I train, they again twist their faces into a look of incredulity. For me, training for triathlons is a matter of having fun and being a kid again. The three skills of triathlon are those of pre-adolescence: Swimming, cycling, and running are kids' activities, and now it is acceptable for me as a grown-up to frolic in their playground again.

"Can it really be fun to train for two or three hours a day?" they ask. For me it's the truth—training is the best part of my day. When I train, I don't have to make business decisions about hiring and firing; I don't have to use money shopping or paying bills; I don't have to stay in one place, like at a desk or a home; and I don't have to get bored by the grind. When I train, I let my mind go as much as I do my body. I have some of my most creative moments when I am training, and I am never bored (although I do get tired).

Triathlons are for fun.

Icebergs

It was written well in 1952:

"Not to have confidence in one's own body is to lose confidence in one-self. . . . It is precisely the female athletes, who, being positively interested in their own game, feel themselves less handicapped in comparison with the male." (Simone de Beauvoir, *The Second Sex.*)

Most of us want to be feminine. Most of us want to be athletes. Twenty years ago, if a woman wanted a sports career, she became a physical education teacher. But now it is common to see professional and Olympic female athletes used as inspirational advertising images.

Somewhere between being feminine and athletic there still seems to be a problem: We feel we can't be both, because the two are such opposites that one must suffer for the other. We want to be athletes, which requires that we be tough, aggressive, and forceful, even dominant. But we must submerge our athletic side when we want to be feminine, a role that is understood to be supportive, passive, tender, emotional. What is a woman supposed to be and do?

It's the same problem I have as an Ironwoman competing in the Ironman. All of the T-shirts, award plaques, and prize-money checks that I ever receive read "Ironman," and yet that's not me. There is a large amount of what sports psychologists call "role conflict" involved with being a woman and being called an Ironman.

Women often react to this confusion in one of two ways. On the one hand are the female Ironman winners who wear jewelry and two-piece, high-cut swimsuits for all three events and cross the finish line with a feminine glow. On the other side are the women Ironman winners who are decked out in the highest-tech gear and apparel that make them so fast they cross the finish line shining from sweat.

My resolution of this role conflict and its resultant confusion, what I call the "iceberg complex," is to work on the thawing principle. The woman with the skimpy two-piece and the woman with the high-tech racing gear are acting out the two thawing ends of an iceberg. One doesn't want to be perceived as too tough, and the other as not too feminine, and neither as androgynous. Both choices are equally valid, and there is room for both models of women in athletics today, whereas thirty or forty years ago, there was room for neither. Indeed there are clear signs of improvement: The Women's Sports Foundation undertook research in 1988 that showed 87 percent of today's moms and dads accept the idea that sports are equally important for boys and girls.

Yet the media still cling to the need for women to fit a mold. When reporters interview a female professional triathlete, they often highlight her marital status or how many children she has alongside her race results, the underlying implication being that even though she is an athlete, she is still fulfilling primary roles of wife and mother. Not as often do I read of a male triathlete as "husband and father of three." As the iceberg thaws, the traditional notion of the female as someone's spouse, mother, or daughter dwindles, and she, you, and I become who we really are, sportswomen.

I eagerly wait for it to melt, and know it will happen in my lifetime.

How the Dollar Goes Around

What do you think when you go to make your sports purchase? Take a moment to consider where that hard-earned dollar you've taken out of your budget is going. To the retailer that provided the water stop at a local 5K fun run? To a logo item from a corporation that sponsors a women's race?

Purchase from those companies such as Danskin, Bonne Bell, Subaru, and Avon that actively support women by providing participant sports opportunities for women. These companies take that dollar you just spent and plough a portion back into the women's participant community. Danskin and other companies that support women don't use your money to promote male athletes in headliner spectator sports. They take a woman's dollar and spend it on women's sports.

This is the nature of sports promotion: Take the consumer's dollar and use it to attract more customers using the same methods. If you buy from companies that support only male athletes or sponsor only professional sporting events, you are sending a message to the company that it is justified in doing "business as usual." But you can use this promotional technique to your benefit. Only buy goods that originate from a company that produces, sponsors, and promotes women's events; that's how the dollar goes around.

Sports is a $60 billion industry in the United States—larger than the auto, petroleum, lumber, or air transportation sectors of the U.S. economy. When women gained the opportunity to play sports under Title IX, the active female consumer became a driving force for a major cultural revolution in the nature of the American woman. In 1972 only one in twenty-seven high school girls played sports. That figure today is one in three. The active female is now a hot new participant segment of the sports market whose size is equal to the relatively stagnant men's market for sporting goods and apparel. Since 1991 women have outpurchased men in athletic shoes and apparel. You have power as one woman to make a difference in many other women's sports opportunities by simply making an informed purchase decision. I advocate making your dollar go around to your community, a community of active, participant sportswomen. In time, your buying power will be heard even louder and stronger.

Getting Older Means Getting Better

Undoubtedly, women (and men) experience major physical changes that affect their athletic performance as they age. And after a dozen years of racing as an Ironwoman in Ironmans, I set a personal best time of ten hours and forty-two minutes, fifteen minutes faster than I have ever raced before. It proved to me that I am getting older and better.

There is no question that getting faster doesn't go on forever. Yet the midpoint in life, formerly around the age of forty, is being pushed further toward the age of fifty, as we live active lifestyles in healthful environments, supported by proper food and medical care. But, on the average, at the age of fifty (in the Western world, fifty-one years), women begin menopause.

Menopause is a natural phenomenon: Menstruation stops and your hormone levels change. There are certain accompanying changes as well, one of which may be osteoporosis, the loss of bone density. Still, you can do a good deal to allay this condition: certain exercises (weight-bearing activities such as running are highly beneficial), nutritional supplements, and lifestyle changes that can prevent significant bone loss. Training can also reduce the symptoms of depression, insomnia, and anxiety, which are associated with menopause.

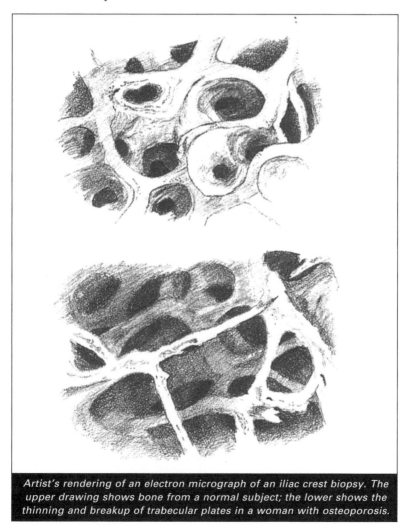

Artist's rendering of an electron micrograph of an iliac crest biopsy. The upper drawing shows bone from a normal subject; the lower shows the thinning and breakup of trabecular plates in a woman with osteoporosis.

Once you hit menopause, you will have to make a decision on hormone-replacement therapies as well. A woman whom I admire for her commitment to a lifetime of training and racing once said to me, "I want more research on the effects of aging on athletic women. I have read everything I can find, and there is little really known about the influences of hormone replacement on the effects of aging in women and on most parameters of athletics."

She's right.

It is known that after the onset of menopause, women tend to have higher cholesterol levels and proportional drops in the "good" type of cholesterol (known as HDL) in their bloodstream, and both these symptoms are risk factors of heart disease. On the positive side, it has also been shown that physical training programs can result in a relative increase of HDL levels, as well as lower cholesterol levels overall.

For those who are past their midpoint and considering starting a triathlon program, I urge you to begin training. Not only are the psychological, physiological, and social benefits important, but also the excitement of a new challenge can make it worth your while to take the triathlon adventure ride.

You're never too old to start something new. Even though some people retire from life at age fifty and while away their time in a recliner, why should you?

For me, aging is a secret athletic weapon, because each year I understand so much more about (and learn so much more from) the sports experience. If you ask me why I did so well at the Japan Ironman one year as a master's competitor, I would tell you it's because I now know what it takes to excel in a way I've never known before. It wasn't my heart and lungs that made it possible; it was being the best at who I am—a triathlete and a woman.

A Special Note to Tri-Parents

After childbirth, tri-fitness is redefined. Luckily, you're the one who gets to write the new definition of your own fitness, so you can either give up training and wallow in soap operas and chocolate or get with a program. Taking care of your physical self *is* taking care of your kids. It's money in the bank for life's little energy drains, such as the sitter who makes a mess or the out-of-town trip you have to take. Moreover, you must have energy to keep pace with the kids' shenanigans, energy that comes from good health and exercise. Sure, it's extra tough to be a fit mom, but you gave birth didn't you? That's how tough you are.

Here are a few tips for training as a parent:

1. *Get the right equipment to train:* You need to invest in a baby jogger for running, backpacks for walking, and bike trailers for cycling.
2. *Get a training partner and alternate training times:* Find another parent as your training partner. While one parent is out, the other watches the children. The children love it, because they are outdoors and they learn the exercise routine (which equates with play to them). If you can't find a fellow parent training partner, advertise for one in a local running or cycling newsletter.
3. *Join a club that provides childcare:* At many athletic clubs, childcare is available. Check before you join.
4. *Enroll your children in sports programs:* At the same time your kids are learning to swim or training with their soccer, basketball, or softball teams, you too can train. I know one professional athlete who brings her bike and track stand to her kid's games!

Relationships

As the offspring of the running revolution, the sport of triathlon had hordes of runners and marathoners learning to cope with their new lifestyle—fitting together a training regimen with other commitments. The relationship statistics from the running population during the 1990s were brutal:

- Male runners married to sedentary females had only a fifty-fifty chance of overcoming marital difficulties.
- Women runners were twice as likely as male runners to reassess their relationships due to sports.
- The divorce rate was three times higher among runners than the national average.
- Sedentary men were jealous of their athletic wives.
- Male runners said it was unimportant whether their wives ran, whereas female runners sought athletic partners.

There are complicated reasons why running may lead to marital and relationship problems, reasons that extend beyond the mere time spent pounding roads and trails. And triathlon, as running's stepchild, is similar enough that it produces noticeable strains on relationships.

There are certainly aspects of triathlon that could contribute to the decay of personal relationships. Triathlon, like running, is a solitary endeavor that can become both self-absorptive and narcissistic. Even if both partners participate, they usually can't be together during triathlon sports.

Training also leads to enhanced self-confidence. This new or increased self-esteem can lead to a questioning of one's choices, among them whether to proceed with a marriage or have children.

Finally, I can't deny that training takes time. The time it takes to train is sometimes the same time that a triathlete would have spent with friends and family. Sadly, the competition for time can be such a fierce battle that when the dust settles there may not be a relationship.

On the other hand, there are aspects of triathlon that can contribute to the growth of personal relationships. Training can lead to stability, commitment, discipline, and tenacity, and getting in shape often results in increased emotional stability, toughness, and flexibility.

Training alone can't make or break a marriage or a relationship or divide a family. However, if training becomes an obsession and dominates life to the exclusion of all else, it's time to do some self-analysis in order to find out what has driven you to such an extreme. Sports should enhance your life, providing you with the riches of health and experience, but it is a monster if it controls you.

The sharing of a lifestyle that includes athletic participation is central to the success of any relationship between athletes over the long run, swim, or bike. Triathlons may strain a healthy relationship, just as they strain a healthy heart—for the good!

About Men

It's tough to break with tradition; some people never can.

In my case, I was taught as my mother was to grow up, marry, have 2.2 children, and live happily ever after. However, thanks to my military-officer father, who raised my three older brothers to be athletes and soldiers, I was also reared as an athlete, because my mom and dad just didn't know any other approach.

It's not hard to understand why more of my fellow athletic sisters aren't lining up at the starting line with me. In my age group, grand master's women (age fifty and up), the majority of females weren't given even the mixed support as children that I had. I must thank each of those master's women for being there. I know what it takes to run against the tide, against the peer-group pressure that requires conformity. I know how hard it is to stand on a beach beside larger and stronger males, scantily clad in your swim-suit. But, with each passing event, we carve a deeper rift in the outmoded tradition of "a woman's place is..." (only you can fill in the rest).

In my first book on triathlons, *Triathlons: A Triple Fitness Sport* (1982), I wanted to open with a discussion of the real problem for most female triathletes: fear, stemming mostly from intimidation. My editor argued that men couldn't imagine the fear that comes from standing next to people who are a minimum of four inches taller than you and forty pounds heavier. Men, he said, could fear only the race, not the racers.

Men, as a sex, view women's lack of participation differently from women. Many believe that since women are not as strong or as fast, since they don't beat men's times, their performance is less important. Men have grown accustomed to (and some prefer) women serving as the support team, in the home and on the playgrounds of triathlon. For them, the woman's place is understood to be behind her man, her athlete. Any other place, such as biking down the road in front of him, may be threatening. Competition or discouragement from significant others is but one of women's barriers to participation.

Do race promoters and the media take women as seriously as men? Here are some facts: In races, women start in waves behind the men. They frequently receive smaller and fewer trophies, and the winners on the awards stage who receive the loudest applause and the most attention are always the top finishers in the men's division. Finally, the photos in the newspaper the next day invariably show the men's winner breaking the tape. If there is a picture of the women's winner, it is typically buried in the back of the article, just as women's results are.

Women themselves can create barriers to their own participation. Many potential female competitors are at races, but they stand on the sidelines as spectators. They watch us, and I wonder what they're thinking. The female spectator dishes out her own brand of peer pressure—she comes to the race to support her man. She helps carry the gear and the kids, takes pictures at the finish line, and brings the post-race food and drinks. She is ready to give the massages, and in return she may receive laurels of praise for her support.

She isn't confused as is the female athlete who bears the dual roles of being "feminine" and being strong and sweaty. The female athlete takes the risk of racing to the finish line and arriving there disheveled and exhausted. And who is there to support her, to bring the kids and the camera, waiting for her to finish?

A woman's real place is wherever she wants it to be, and it is time for everyone to recognize that women's reasons for not being triathletes are different from men's reasons. And it is time to support those women who want to tear down the wall of sexist tradition.

For future females, I hope it won't take a father like mine, who raised his daughter as his fourth son, for a little girl to grow into a triathletic woman.

Men can have a great deal to do with that change.

Predicions for the Future of Women in Triathlons

In 1982 I wrote the first book on our sport, *Triathlons: A Triple Fitness Sport*. In that book I made some predictions on the future of the young event. Here are the ones that have come true:

- Triathlon has become an Olympic sport.
- Triathlon is being viewed by the public as a true, all-around fitness contest.
- Triathletes (mostly male) make hundreds of thousands of dollars in income from the sport.

I hope you can share my vision of what the future may hold, an even larger field of opportunity for women to participate in as I look to the future of women in triathlon:

- *Increased participation.* With the increased acceptance of women in sports and the increased opportunities available to women to be who they are, the ratio of men and women in triathlon is approaching a balance. Women form the largest number of new participants in the single sports of swimming, cycling, and running, so it shouldn't be long before many make the transition to triathlon.
- *Equal opportunities.* Today, a professional woman triathlete makes approximately seventy cents to every dollar that her male counterpart makes—it's about the same with most professions in America. As the value of women's work is recognized and the inalienable right to equal pay for equal work is mandated, a woman should make a dollar for every dollar a man makes.
- *Research.* We're seeing more of how triathlon participation promotes research into the areas of biological differences, physiological changes,

and the aging process. This information will revolutionize the current body of knowledge on athletic performance and women.

• *Front covers.* A woman triathlete will frequently grace the front cover of major sports magazines.

• *Records broken.* Throughout the next decade, new world records will be set in all distances and for all ages of women. The increased pressure from international competition will force higher-quality training that will result in improved performances.

• *Equal media coverage.* Magazine, newspaper, and television coverage of the sport will feature equal emphasis on both the women's and the men's races. Currently, the media treat the women's race as a subcategory of the men's, a second child.

• *Equal respect.* Women's achievements will come to be acknowledged as equal to men's due to an increased understanding and respect for the differences in male and female physiology and resultant performance.

• *Role models.* Women triathletes will become role models for children who admire athletes because of their accomplishments.

These prospects may sound like a dream, but they aren't. They can all come true if there is strong leadership and a commitment to change and progress.

I invite you to join the union of fitness triathletes and make the change happen.

The Sweet Spot

The day before the 1998 Ironman Triathlon World Championships, I was in serious pre-race rest preparation sitting on the beaches of Kona, Hawaii, when I received an e-mail from a couple of business friends of mine. Teresa and Mary have finished the Ironman nine times. They know what it's about. Their e-mail was brief and to the point: "Take no prisoners."

Mary and Teresa knew that for me this race was the big one, and that my goal was to set the grand master's record. They knew that in every race I came from behind and passed all of the other grand master's women. I knew that I would again have to catch my competition during the marathon leg of this race.

The next day, at the start of the marathon, my nemesis had a twenty-eight-minute lead, and I knew that her strength was running. I went after her knowing her lead was substantial.

*Sally Edwards giving a thumbs-up before the start
of one of her Ironman triathlons.*

There came a moment during the marathon when I had reached the point of absolute exhaustion—the high heat and winds had taken their toll. I knew I had to shake the weariness. Slowly, I felt a strange rush of sensation, one difficult to explain. I call it the "sweet spot" in sports.

It was as if everything were coming together and the exhaustion was being let go; it was a feeling of possibility, blended with a sense of hope. I started to feel better—I picked up the pace, and I was joyfully conscious that what was happening was a rare phenomenon.

However, that sweet experience lasted only briefly. Then, one of my close friends and training partners rode by on a moped—she was working as a spotter, reporting rather than racing that day. I asked her how far ahead the woman was that I wanted to beat. My friend said she was about to finish, while I was still miles from the finish line. It hurt to hear.

Still, I took strength from my previous moments of sweetness and decided that I would give it my best, because in sports no one knows the outcome until the last competitor crosses the finish line. I also believe that in sports your competition is ultimately with yourself, a finishing clock, and a course, not the people around you.

The woman ahead of me beat me by nine minutes in eleven hours of racing. She took me as her prisoner. Yet I took that moment—the sweet spot —as mine. Both the victory and the defeat were what I made of them, and I left the experience with hope for the future.

The sweet spot is about the indomitable human spirit. For women, our spirit is expanding as acceptance grows of females as fully capable human beings, with every right to access all avenues. We must be connected to the truths and desires of our own spirits if we are to live a life of sweet spots. And, conversely, following your sweet spots can help you find your own internal life-affirming spirit. By all means, find it and live it, and take very good care of yourself in the process.

FEEDING THE FIRES

The question invariably asked by people interested in health and fitness is this: "What is the best diet for me? What combination of fuels will best clean out my pipes, rev up the engines, and fire the motor that takes me through the rigorous physical and mental demands of my typical day?" Nutritional experts, health faddists, and successful experienced athletes expound at length on the subject of nutrition and diet, bombarding us with a mass of conflicting theories and recommendations. It's no wonder we're confused.

Optimum diet can be defined as that particular combination of foods that stimulates the body to perform with maximum comfort and efficiency in a predictable variety of situations. A well-balanced diet is necessary for everyone, but it is particularly important for individuals in highly stressful situations; such as the female triathlete. How can we gauge the relative values of different food types in this search to find the best fuels? We can learn, perhaps, by the example of another culture.

The Hunzas, who live in the Karakoram mountain range of the Himalayas in Pakistan, count 2,875 centenarians per million, whereas the ratio in the United States is only 8 per million, one of the lowest in the world. Furthermore, the Hunzas exist apparently cancer-free, according to a recent study by the United Nations Educational, Scientific, and Cultural Organization

(UNESCO). The Hunzas work strenuously in an agricultural community, eating a diet that has been relatively unchanged for centuries, primarily one of nuts, fruits, vegetables, and a variety of whole grains. Preservatives, additives, processing procedures, engineering of nutrient content, and chemicals have no place in the Himalayan diet, nor do meat and refined sugar. It would be simplistic to attribute the society's unusually high level of wellness to diet and exercise alone, but good nutrition and exercise clearly have played a significant role in producing generations of healthy, vital, long-lived Hunzas.

Despite the diversity of their individual theories, health experts generally agree on one basic formula for overall good health. Compare the parts of this formula with the lifestyle you are living and see how they match:

Balanced nutrition + physical activity + quality sleep + fresh air + good genes + moderate exposure to sunlight + low stress + mentally active =
Best changes for good health

The Hunza society is a living testament to this lifestyle; the core of their nutritional program might well be adapted to the programs of other active individuals. If the body is a temple, as the great teachers say, we should not treat it as if it were the local dump.

Triathletes should closely evaluate their eating habits, monitoring the amount, type, and nutritional value of the foods they ingest. Probably the most optimum diet for a triathlete is one that will both tune up the engine and turn it on toward high performance. After thirty years of training and racing, I have found some simple criteria that help me unravel the confusion caused by obsolete nutritional theories, commercial-interested confusion among the experts, and the lack of reliable information. Before I eat any food, I ask myself "What will it give me, and what will it cost me?"

Food gives the body a source of fuel that it can burn for energy and provides certain nutritional benefits (e.g., protein to repair muscle tissue). However, food can cost the body. It may provide empty (non-nutritious) calories, or it may be difficult and/or take a long time to digest. To use an economic metaphor, there is a cost-benefit ratio that applies to the act of eating. It makes sense, therefore, that the food we put into our incredible machines must pay some dividends—that it gives us more than it costs us.

Average Daily Caloric Consumption

The number of calories you take in and how you blend those calories are personal choices. By starting a triathlon training program, you will probably be burning more total calories in your day. Your energy requirements depend primarily on your training load, or how much exercise you complete. A rough estimate of caloric costs and therefore energy requirements of training is that you will expend approximately 500–700 calories per hour if you are training at a moderate intensity, or at 60–80 percent of your maximum heart rate (heart zones 2 and 3).

Your total daily caloric cost, or daily energy expenditure (EE), is the sum of these three factors:

$$EE_{sum} = \text{basal metabolism} + \text{physical activity} + \text{digestion} =$$
Total number of calories burned daily

To burn more calories, you must stoke up your basal metabolic rate, increase the amount of your physical activity, and eat nutritiously. To increase your metabolic rate, also known as your burn rate, you must change your body composition, the ratio of fat weight to fat-free weight. Triathlon training increases your muscle mass and therefore increases your burn rate at rest. Triathlon training also increases your caloric output because you are exercising more. The final part of the EE_{sum} equation is the caloric cost of digestion, which is based on the types and kinds of foods you eat. Each food has a caloric cost of digestion that can be determined.

After years of manipulating this calories-out side of the energy-balancing equation, I have found that using a calorie-allowance system works for me. The next table will help you to determine how many calories per day you can allocate for yourself based on your physical activity level. Also, notice how increasing the physical activity part of the formula makes enormous differences in your daily burn rate:

Eating to Feed Your Metabolism

As you learn to fine-tune your diet, you will notice that your body begins to regard food as fuel, the fuel that makes your muscles operate efficiently. Muscle burns primarily glucose and glycogen. Research shows that the muscle tissues consume 90 percent of all calories burned in a day's activities. It would seem reasonable, then, to feed our muscles those fuels they can

DAILY CALORIE ALLOWANCE FOR ACTIVE TRIATHLETES AND SEDENTARY WOMEN						
Your Weight (in pounds)	Competitive Triathlete	Highly Active	Active	Moderately Active	Low Active	Completely Sedentary
80	1,600	1,440	1,280	1,120	960	800
90	1,800	1,620	1,440	1,260	1,080	900
100	1,900	1,800	1,600	1,400	1,200	1,000
110	2,000	1,980	1,760	1,540	1,320	1,100
120	2,200	2,160	1,920	1,680	1,440	1,200
130	2,400	2,340	2,080	1,820	1,560	1,300
140	2,600	2,520	2,240	1,960	1,680	1,400
150	2,800	2,700	2,400	2,100	1,800	1,500
160	3,000	2,880	2,560	2,240	1,920	1,600
170	3,200	3,060	2,720	2,380	2,040	1,700
180	3,400	3,240	2,880	2,520	2,160	1,800
190	3,600	3,420	3,200	2,660	2,280	1,900
200	3,800	3,600	3,360	2,800	2,400	2,000

make the best use of—complex carbohydrates, which are the source of muscle sugars

Source of Calories

When I eat, I do so to meet my metabolic needs for supplying my fat-free mass, my muscles and essential tissues. My muscles prefer carbohydrates, so I feed them just that. I don't eat to feed my fat; my body already stores sufficient amounts of fat without my encouraging it to store more. Protein, needed to rebuild or resynthesize tissues, is required only in small quantities. The recommended breakdown among these three principle food sources for percentage of daily caloric intake (plus or minus 5 percent) is the formula I use as a guide:

- Complex carbohydrates: 60–65 percent
- Protein: 10–15 percent
- Dietary fat: 20–25 percent

By maintaining a diet that is balanced and full of nutrients and that consists of a healthy ratio of fats, proteins, and complex carbohydrates, you are feeding your engine a blend that results in a high-octane fuel.

Tips on Nutrition and Eating Habits

Here are a few everyday, sensible nutritional guidelines that I follow:

- *Eat whole foods.* This means foods that are complete, unfragmented, unrefined, and neither fortified nor enriched. Fill your grocery cart with nuts, spinach, tofu, fresh fruit, beans, tomatoes, rice, barley, and so on.
- *Eat complex carbohydrates.* These foods form the gasoline that fires up our motors—grains, breads, and potatoes. They digest more slowly than simple sugars—cookies, ice cream, and cake—and do not produce a rapid rise and fall in blood-sugar level.
- *Eat modest amounts of protein.* The old-time nutritionist said, "Eat what you are made of." The modern-day nutritionist says, "Eat what gives you energy—complex carbohydrates."
- *Eat living foods.* Such foods as apples, bananas, carrots, sunflower seeds, and sprouts are examples of living foods because they are in their original state usually when you eat them.
- *Eat unprocessed foods.* These are foods with no chemicals, preservatives, or sweeteners added, or those that have not been altered mechanically or by cooking or freezing. Avoid chemical additives. Apply this simple test: If you can't wash it, don't eat it.
- *Eat unpackaged foods.* Canned, jarred, sealed, or frozen food must be adulterated for containment. Choose the same foods in their natural state.
- *Eat foods in combination.* To assimilate and digest foods optimally, present them to your stomach in balanced combination.
- *Eat to feed your muscles, not your fat.* Eat only as much as you need, not as much as you might want. Fat is nonworking tissue, so there is little need to feed it. Eat for physical energy, not for emotional comfort.
- *Chew your food well and slowly.* The saliva in your mouth begins the chemical breakdown of the food; this is the start of the digestive process.
- *Breathe while you chew.* Breathing will enhance the flavor and contribute to overall satisfaction and satiation. You might discover that you don't eat as much quantity when your breathing helps you eat with focus on the present moment.
- *Eat in a relaxed, pleasant environment.* Don't combine eating with loud, disruptive activities, such as animated conversation or noisy music. Concentrate on and enjoy the process of eating.
- *Be aware that food nutrients are easily lost.* Eat fresh foods and cook them lightly, if at all.

• *Eat when you're hungry,* not just because it's the conventional time for a meal three times a day. Let real hunger be a guide to when and how much and how often you eat. Small amounts more frequently may be a better eating pattern for you.

If you wish to lose weight, eat very little after 6:00–7:00 at night. Since you are less likely to be physically active then, the chances are greater that any food you eat will be stored in adipose tissues (fat cells).

Food Supplements

An area of heated debate with regard to diet today is the issue of food supplements. Some people feel that if you eat multiple balanced meals a day, you will receive all of the MDR (minimum daily requirements) of vitamins, minerals, and other nutrients needed by your body. On the other hand, the pill industry lobbies fiercely to raise those MDR levels and advertises extensively to get you to feel that you must swallow a one-a-day vitamin.

As an endurance athlete, I frequently stress my incredible energy machine to its capacity. Then I demand that my immune system resist breakdown and rebuild my body to higher levels of work capacity. This stress-and-rebuild regimen requires more from my system than that of the average sedentary or unfit woman. Many women add to the stress-recovery cycle other substances that truly damage your body: toxins such as cigarette smoke, overindulgence in alcohol, and packaged/canned/fast foods. Complicating this is the fact that many sedentary women lack natural and daily stress reducers, such as hobbies, exercise, and joyful pastimes. Still others struggle with overexposure to computers, electronic toys, and television.

It thus seems logical that the minimal daily nutritional requirements would be different for the average person and the triathlete. In this situation, I suggest you pose the nutritional test: "What will it give me, and what will it cost me?" Intake of food supplements above the MDR passes this nutritional test. The benefit is to strengthen the immune system, and the cost is the financial price of the supplements. Is it worth it? Probably.

At a minimum, I recommend that you supplement your diet with antioxidants. I remember the ingredients of my antioxidant cocktail by their acronym, ACE, which represents vitamins A, C, and E. Most multivitamins have all three ingredients, but check for the amount of vitamin C and vitamin E, as the dosage is usually too low.

Listen to the nutritional needs of your body by paying attention to the signals it gives. I like to keep a nutritional performance journal to analyze those messages. For example, if a food or vitamin improves my diet, I use it; if not, I don't. After all, eating is one of the few variables you can control. Eating well is certainly worth the expenditure in time to maximize the benefits by eating with intelligence.

Eating for Performance

While your arms are thrusting through the water or your legs spinning down the road or your feet pounding toward the finish line, your stomach may be in one of many states: quiet, hungry, upset, in contractions, or in the unpleasant process of emptying itself. What your stomach can handle, other people's stomachs perhaps can't. Sports nutrition is unique for each individual, so don't compare yourself with others. Rather, follow your instincts as to what your body needs.

Pre-race Meal

The pre-race meal should be composed of foods that you can keep moving through your GI (gastrointestinal tract) during the swim. If you are like some people, food in the stomach during exercise causes nausea, probably because of the "nervous-stomach syndrome." Nervous stomach is caused by the release of hydrochloric acid into the stomach combined with the fact that during competition blood normally sent to the stomach is shunted to the working muscles to provide them with oxygen and nutrients. The result of an upset stomach during the race is impaired breathing, flatulence, and diarrhea.

Experiment to find out which foods sit best in your stomach. Generally, two hours before my wave starts, I eat a light, complex-carbohydrate meal of about 500 calories. My pre-race meal might include a muffin or bagel, a banana or energy bar, whole-grain toast, and pancakes, but no juice because it is usually high in acid. Foods high in protein are generally a bad choice, since they remain in your stomach a long time. I avoid dairy products for forty-eight hours before the race; they tend to result in loose bowels, unpleasant at best. Your pre-race meal should be sufficiently substantial to eliminate both weakness and hunger. Eating two hours before the race ensures that your stomach and upper bowels are relatively empty during the race and that your bloodstream has carbohydrates to deliver to the working muscles. Here's a tip: I'm a coffee drinker and I enjoy a cup of coffee during this meal, as that also helps my bowels to eliminate everything before the race begins.

During-the-Race Meal

If you know you will finish a triathlon or a training workout in less than two hours, you don't need to read this section. For most people, eating during a short race or training session provides little energy benefit. For triathlons that last longer than two to three hours, eating during the race is as important as eating before it.

Again, each of us is different in our training and nutritional needs. I've had my fair share of involuntary stomach emptying while racing and have developed the following criteria for acceptable food to eat during a race:

- Food that is in season, low in fat, and free of dairy products
- Food that is easy to chew
- Food that tastes good
- Food that is not monotonous but has variety
- Food that does not bring on dehydration
- Food that can be assimilated rapidly, so that the muscles can make use of the energy
- Food that is in liquid form

I know that what I eat during the race can contribute substantially to my performance. Another way of saying this is that eating properly during the race will result in my enjoying my performance and finishing faster. Therefore, I want to store my muscle glycogen (sugars stored within the muscle cells) and begin a fat-metabolism cycle as early as possible. To encourage this fat-metabolism cycle, I even talk myself into a nutritional mantra, repeating "burn fat, burn fat, burn fat."

I don't start eating during the race until I'm out of the water and onto my bike. For long races, I store foods in T1 (swim-to-bike transition) that I carry with me to eat during the bike leg. Some that work best for me are pulped fruits (bananas, apples, or strawberries). They can be easily packaged and swallowed quickly, and they meet all of my criteria: variety, flavor, chewability, complex carbohydrates, easy on the stomach (but a little difficult sometimes on the bowels). Though not as enjoyable, liquid meals have been an excellent energy source for me during my Ironman distance races.

During extremely hot-weather races, I like watermelon diced into small pieces with a little salt on top.

After experimentation, I've found that it is easier on the GI tract to eat small amounts frequently rather than large amounts infrequently. Rather than eating an entire energy bar at once, I spread it into several bites during the race. I supplement this energy source with a hard rock candy that dissolves slowly in my mouth (seven minutes for a small piece). This gradual intake of calories from hard candy helps to minimize the massive changes in blood-sugar level that occur with high-intensity exercise, and it reduces the pancreas's response of dumping insulin into the body in massive amounts after you've eaten the high concentrations of complex sugars found in energy bars and gels.

Some triathletes perform well eating special liquid meals, which were originally developed for hospital patients unable to eat solid foods. Liquid meals are high in calories, provide for hydration, and are easily ingested. Do not confuse them with instant powdered meals or meal supplements, as these are generally mixed with milk and are high in fat and protein. Liquid meals are convenient, easily digested, soothing to a nervous stomach, high in carbs, and low in fats. Some brand-name liquid foods are Ensure (Ross Products), Sustacal and Sustagen (Mead Johnson), Power Dream (Imagine Foods), and Nutriment. Or you can make your own concoction and not have to worry about the additives in these packaged, engineered foods.

One last tip: Ask race management in advance if there will be food at the aid stations and, if so, what kind and where, so that you can plan your nutritional needs. I advised you earlier in the chapter to eat when you're hungry; that rule doesn't hold during a race. Heat and exhaustion extinguish the feeling of hunger, so eat by the clock.

Fluids

Your need for fluids during a training session or a race is totally individual. Your body depends on proper hydration for normal metabolic function. A typical 150-pound woman carries approximately 90 pounds of water on board, and half of that is stored in the muscle tissue. Your body is a water reservoir; you need to keep it full.

During the race and hard training, fluid intake is crucial. The quantities you drink depend on how much you sweat, which depends on individual conditions:

• Temperature
• Humidity
• Your current training state
• Intensity of your exertion
• Your individual sweat propensities

Among these factors that determine your fluid requirements are your ability to sweat (if you sweat a great deal, you must drink more fluids) and the relative humidity (as the humidity increases, your ability to be cooled by sweating decreases). Water poured over the body during the race will help cool you as well. If the racecourse lacks shade and the sun is blazing, your need to drink more increases. Wear a hat with a bill that will help cool you, especially if you keep it wet. Wearing white or light-colored clothing will help, too. Drinking chilled fluids will also lower your core body temperature—but use caution, because cold liquids can give some people severe abdominal cramps.

How much water loss you experience is critical to your continued performance. For every 1 percent of body weight lost in water, your blood volume drops by 2.4 percent. With a water loss of 4 percent, your performance is reduced considerably, and there is a marked reduction in strength and endurance. A 6 percent water loss results in exhaustion, but it should never come to this because you are constantly filling your water reservoir.

Hyperhydration, or loading on fluids in advance of a race, is a practice I follow when the event is staged in hot climates. If you are hyperhydrated, you should weigh more on the morning of a race because you are carrying more stored liquids on board your system.

You need to stay hydrated during your training and racing because water loss reduces your ability to perform. When you become dehydrated, your blood thickens because there is less water in the bloodstream. This limits the bloodstream's ability to transport nutrients and oxygen. And as you sweat, mineral loss occurs. Therefore, it is important to replace both the water loss as well as the mineral loss by drinking an electrolyte-replacement drink if you are training or racing in hot climates.

Before the advent of electrolyte-replacement drinks, we made our own concoctions adding table salt, bee's honey, and other secret ingredients to water. These are less expensive, but you might prefer the commercial products. There are dozens of commercial drinks available today that are a combination of liquid fluids and minerals, such as Gatorade, Ultima, Accelerade (PacificHealth Laboratories), and Revenge (Champion Nutrition).

Composition of Sweat and Mineral Loss During a Race (in milligrams per liter of sweat)					
Mineral	**Amount**	**Mineral**	**Amount**	**Mineral**	**Amount**
Sodium	1,200	Phosphate	15	Chloride	1,000
Zinc	1.2	Potassium	300	Lactic acid	1,500
Calcium	160	Iron	1.2	Magnesium	36
Uric acid	700	Sulphate	25	Vitamin C	50

It is best to drink water on a timed schedule rather than wait until you feel thirsty. The body's hydrostat does not always tell you how much you need. As with food, fluid is better taken more frequently in smaller amounts rather than less frequently in larger amounts. How much and how often you drink depends entirely on your needs, your ability to utilize fluids, your body size, and the ambient temperature and humidity. When I train in the heat, I carry a handheld eight-ounce water bottle. On long training sessions, I refill frequently or carry a water hydration pack with fluid-filled bladders. During the race, I take water at every aid station, consuming four to six fluid ounces, and hope that the stations are spaced about twenty minutes apart. To cool my "radiator," I pour water over my head (though I try not to get water in my running shoes because wet shoes invariably give me blisters).

At the end of the race, the body needs fluids and rest. Water is absorbed faster than any other fluid (it takes about twenty minutes to absorb juice). If the weather is particularly hot and dry, you will need to drink two to three glasses of water almost immediately after crossing the finish line. Then slowly drink some fruit juice or commercial electrolyte-replacement solution. The water will replace the lost fluids and increase your blood volume; the juice will replace lost electrolytes (sodium, potassium, and magnesium). Next, do some heavy-duty resting. Massage will help, as will hot and cold whirlpools.

Ergogenic Aids

By definition, an ergogenic aid is anything introduced into the body that provides performance enhancement. Among the substances and nutrients that can influence performance capacity are electrolyte or sport drinks, vitamins, caffeine, aspirin, creatine, amino acids, L-carnitine, substances with an immune-modulating effect (medicine or drugs), and energy bars and gels.

Most triathletes who use ergogenic aids do so to help improve their ability to train harder (load tolerance) and for regeneration (recovery between training sessions). Consumption of these substances is advantageous in these situations. However, all active substances or medicines/drugs having a clear performance-enhancing or -influencing effect that give an athlete an advantage are banned and placed on a doping list, which is determined by international sports governing federations. Consumption of these aids is a doping activity that not only presents a health risk but also is unethical. Items on the doping list include stimulants, narcotics, anabolic substances, diuretics, growth hormones, banned methods (such as blood doping), alcohol, and other substance groups.

Update on Diets for Weight Loss or Weight Management

Many women are lured to cross-training because they want to achieve weight loss. Research shows that the best long-term solution for those seeking this result is a combination of factors, principally changing diet and increasing energy expenditure (EE). Of these two sides of the energy-balancing equation, changing the type and nature of the energy input (calories consumed) can play a significant role in reducing body weight.

The impact of fat on weight loss has recently received a great deal of attention. Five recent independent research studies show that lowering the amount of fat in your diet results in spontaneous reduction in body weight. Likewise, continuing to maintain a low-fat diet may also be important for keeping weight off: The research shows that "a 10% reduction in fat intake can have a significant impact on energy balance and body weight over the long-term."[1] Current scientific evidence indicates that the fat content of diet directly affects body weight and that reducing fat intake to no more than 30 percent of total daily calories results in improvement in body weight.

The flip side of the equation is energy expenditure, or the total amount of calories you burn in your daily life. Again, the scientific evidence suggests that the combination of changes in diet linked with increased exercise is the most effective behavioral approach for weight loss. Key to keeping weight off is a regular workout program, which is one of the best predictors of long-term weight maintenance.

Setting weight goals is important, as is learning about problem solving, social supports, goal setting, stimulus control, and behavioral skills to enhance the effectiveness of a weight-loss program. The American College of Sports Medicine recommends that the target amount of weight loss should be a 5–10 percent reduction in body weight followed by a maintenance program. This target has been found to be realistic and sufficient to improve health dramatically as well as to prevent disease risks. For example, a 180-pound woman following these prudent guidelines would set a goal of losing 9–18 pounds.

Today, you have the advantage that you can make weight-loss decisions based on scientific facts, not fads and hype. Neither exercise nor diet alone is sufficient for most people to achieve weight loss. Rather, with a combination of the two and with emotional and other support mechanisms, women can successfully lose weight and have more energy. I know of no better way to achieve these goals than by staying active with swimming, cycling, and running and by eating nutrient-dense foods.

Good Nutrition as a Lifestyle

Proper nutrition is essential for health maintenance and fitness. This is of even greater significance if you are training for triathlons, because you are exposing your body to positive physical strain that results in fitness improvement.

Many star triathletes feed their fires with junk food and still win races. They believe that the body is a garbage disposal—that when foods are broken down, the body will take what it needs and eliminate the rest. Some even succeed with this philosophy. These athletes conclude that speed, strength, and stamina—not carrots—make champions.

This philosophy is badly flawed. We owe it to ourselves to live life the best we can. If we are not willing to settle for junk living, we certainly should not settle for junk food. So take a hard look at your eating habits, find out what works for you as an individual, and adapt that into your individualized nutritional eating program.

The next consideration—and in the long run, the most important one—is your health. For me, health is more than merely the absence of disease. It is a positive state of being that pervades our minds and bodies, enabling us to live long, productive, active, and energetic lives. The food we eat should make a positive contribution to that state of being. Eating, like everything else, should be an integral part of life. That is what this book is about—making sports and nutrition second nature, our lifestyle, not just an afterthought in our lives.

Finally, take a moment to consider your physical and emotional performance. If you are a performance-motivated woman triathlete, you want to extend your athletic career, your performance lifespan. My goal is to continue racing until I'm 100 years old—and to do that I know I need to pace myself. Otherwise, the competitive years for each of us may be relatively few. If you are in the midst of those few peak years and special performance-based races, you owe it to yourself to act on the best nutritional and diet information available. Clearly, that information says that you should put the best possible fuel into your incredible energy machine. Socrates said that others lived to eat, while he ate to live. For the performance triathlete, perhaps you should improve on his maxim by saying, "Other women eat to live, while I eat to perform."

Notes
1. American College of Sports Medicine Position Stand, "Appropriate Intervention Strategies for Weight Loss and Prevention of Weight Regain for Adults," *Medicine and Science in Sports and Exercise,* vol. 33, no. 12 (December 2001), p. 2147.

TOOLS OF THE TRIATHLON GAME

Triathlons synthesize three sports. If you want to maximize performance and minimize risk of injury, choosing equipment for each event is as important as training. In selecting your gear, consider what is needed to participate safely and successfully in each. As in other sports, there are fanatics who will swim only in a certain brand of suit, pedal only with a specific bike fork, or run only in a shoe made for pronators. At the other extreme is the woman who ignores the value of the right equipment, confident that fitness is everything and that the tools of the game are of little importance.

I knew little about equipment during my first triathlon in 1979, a short one staged in Davis, California. It began with the run, my specialty. I strode off in high-fashion racing gear. Winning the foot leg, I hopped helmetless onto my ten-speed clunker and began pedaling furiously, taking myself to heart zone 5 (red-lining) in a matter of moments. I soon heard that sound. It hits you right over the left shoulder, the whoosh as a hot cyclist on a fine racing machine passes you, moving with such smooth quickness that the air flow is barely audible.

At the lake I dismounted from my bike and its painful saddle and stripped to my swimsuit, which hadn't seen service since my college days fifteen years earlier. Gingerly entering the frigid water, I immediately started to chill. No goggles, no swim cap, no wetsuit, no experience—it sapped my heat. After one lap of a double-loop course, I edged my bone-chilled frame to the side of the lake and spent an hour shivering and vowing, "As soon as I get warm, I'll swim that last lap." I never kept that vow. The cold drained my will. I DNF (did not finish) my first triathlon.

Choosing equipment is difficult because of the many manufacturers, the controversies about what is most suitable, the wide range of costs, the constant changes in design, and the triathlete's individual needs. To attack your decision, analyze each sport, make a grocery list of gear, decide on your budget and your true needs, and slowly accumulate the tools of the triathlon game.

Choosing a Pool

Here's a list of variables to compare when deciding on a swimming pool:

- Cost of membership or admittance fees
- Width of the lap lanes
- Use of land dividers
- Proximity to home or work
- Shape of the pool (avoid the kidney-shaped ones)
- Indoor or outdoor facilities
- Times open for individuals for lap swimming
- Times reserved for master's swim groups
- Cleanliness
- Traffic
- Frills: weight room, whirlpool, sauna, and so

Swimming

Ideally, swim training should be held in a pool for interval sessions and in a lake or ocean for open-water workouts. You don't need to move to San Diego or dig a hole in your backyard, however; swimming space is available at low cost. Pools, along with their showers and locker room facilities, vary in quality, so take time to shop for a good one. If you can find a fifty-meter pool, try it, because you can get long stretches of swim training without turns. If not, a twenty-five-yard short-course pool is available at most YWCAs, swim clubs, health clubs, public recreation areas, park departments, and schools. As a last choice, consider the smaller pools found at hotels or a friend's backyard, though these aren't very satisfactory because of the frequent turns you must make.

You may prefer to work out solo during the least crowded periods of recreational lap-swim hours, or you may want an organized workout with other swimmers and a timing clock. Either way, consider buying a swim coach's time for several sessions. A swim coach can provide invaluable advice on how to improve your stroke mechanics, a technique all of us can use help with. Find a coach who knows how to identify your biomechanics and communicate corrections effectively. The pinnacle of training is if a coach can do a video analysis of your style, but few coaches have the necessary sophisticated underwater cameras, and such training is by no means a requirement.

These days, swimming in the nude is a sensual delight reserved mostly for dolphins. Triathletes must wear swimsuits in public, though the suits make few concessions to modesty as they become more daring. Nevertheless, their modern designs and materials reduce the effect of their presence, even visually, and even enhance performance. The latest in swimsuits is usually previewed at the Olympic Games, where swim records fall because of improved science: science in training, in design and materials of suits, and in biomechanics.

Swim Equipment

The equipment needed for all three events of the triathlon can add up to a formidable list, not only in quantity but cost as well. For swimming, fortunately, most items with the exception of the swimsuit and goggles are to an extent optional.

Swimsuit

When buying a suit, try it on and practice a dry-land version of the freestyle with a few kicking motions to see if it fits comfortably on contracting muscles. It should not slip or rub. The shoulder straps should allow for about a 2-inch stretch when pulled toward the ears.

Lycra suits are standard racing apparel for competitive triathletes. The Lycra stretch fabric adheres tightly to the skin, preventing drag as well as providing some breast and stomach support. There are different cuts and styles — some suits even have padded crotches, which are useful on the bike and run stages of a triathlon. The suits dry quickly and should last one to two years without stretching out and losing their shape.

Swim Goggles

Though goggles improve vision, their main purpose is to reduce eye irritation. Cheap or ill-kept ones can be irritating — they may fog frequently, leak, or slip off the face. It's best to buy expensive goggles and eliminate the hassles. Most goggles require numerous adjustments until they fit; it may take a week to get them correctly adjusted.

Pull Buoys

Usually cylindrical pieces of styrofoam, pull buoys allow you to rest your legs by floating them in a natural position, as you isolate your upper body during area-specific workouts. Pulling drills can also be conducted by using small black inner tubes, called "pulling tubes," around your ankles. They provide greater resistance in training than do pull buoys, since they aren't buoyant and therefore don't hold your legs up.

Kickboards

Usually made from styrofoam-like materials, kickboards are used to condition your legs and improve the biomechanics of your kick. Kickboards are held with your hands and arms, allowing them to rest, as you isolate the leg movement.

Swim Fins

Used as a training aid, swim fins (such as Zoomers) can increase the flexibility of your ankles, build the strength of your quadriceps (thigh muscles), and provide a tougher workout by increasing your cardiovascular load. They also allow you to go longer, since you are using your legs more, and thus your arms don't tire as fast. This can help you get up to the yardage or time you need in the pool to prepare for a triathlon, although fins are not allowed during the race.

Hand Paddles

These are usually flat pieces of thin plastic, with surgical tubing attached in order to secure your hands to the paddle. They are used as training devices, which improve your arm stroke by forcing your hands and arms into the correct stroking pattern. Paddles also increase stroke force, but some research shows that with overuse they may cause shoulder tendinitis.

Pace Clock

This is a large clock with a sweep second hand that is used for timing your repeats and determining your departure times. Pace clocks are usually mounted on the wall or seated on the pool deck.

Defogging Solutions

Swim goggles fog easily, but this can be prevented in a number of ways.

You can put either a commercial defogging solution or saliva on the inside of them, or buy antifog goggles, which are also available.

Heart Rate Monitor

This moderately expensive device (available for as little as $50, although the ones with more options sell for upward of $250) provides an accurate way to measure your heart rate. Some can even store times and training zones for each segment of your workout ("splits"), so that you can time your repeats and, at the end of the set, download and replay your exact splits. For more information, see Chapter 2, "Heart Zones Training," or the appendix at the end of the book on buying an HRM.

Biking

Biking entails an abundance of technique and equipment and has considerable accompanying jargon. With so much to know, the details can become confusing. To the aficionado cyclist, buying bike gear is simple: Get the finest wheels attached to an ultralight frame, make sure the name Shimano or Campagnolo is stamped on all the other components, drop on a pair of aerobars, get a bike monitor (a combination HRM and bike computer that provides HR data as well as bike speed, cadence, distance traveled, and other features), and then set up the bike aerodynamically. All this technical babel can be intimidating to people accustomed to less complicated sports such as running. Not only must you buy an expensive thoroughbred machine, but you also must custom design it, fit it, adjust it, understand it, conform to it, power it, and baby-sit it. This is only partly true.

I suggest that one of your first biking purchases be a good bicycling book. There are plenty available today that are written for the woman cyclist and consumer; I'd recommend one of the following:

- *The Female Cyclist,* Gale Bernhardt
- *A Woman's Guide to Bikes and Biking,* Julie Harrell
- *A Woman's Guide to Cycling,* Susan Weaver
- *The Heart Rate Monitor Book for Cyclists,* Sally Reed and Sally Edwards
- *The Heart Rate Monitor Workbook for Cyclists,* Sally Reed and Sally Edwards

These books give detailed information on everything from selecting a bike geared for you to training methodologies to information on where to shop. Read up in advance of heading for your local bike specialty shop so that you can be armed with information. Tell the local owner your situation and your budget and ask for his or her suggestions; in short, be a savvy buyer.

The Bike: Your Primary Tool

Off-the-Rack or Custom Bikes

I covered several features of bikes in Chapter 4 but will review some important ones here that are of particular interest to triathletes new to the bike scene. First, a bicycle has two parts: the frame and the components. When you purchase a stock off-the-floor bike, you get the frame and the components together unless your shop will agree to trade-ins on stock components. The standard recreational ten- (or fifteen- or eighteen-) speed stock bikes are constructed of different types of materials: metal or plastics. They can range from as low as $300 (which you want to avoid for safety reasons) up to several thousand dollars. Basic components include wheels, derailleur, crank set, handlebars (or aerobars), brakes, saddle, electronics, and accessories.

The geometry of frame design varies with your choice of bike: touring bikes, racing bikes, cross bikes, and tri bikes. Each has its advantages and disadvantages, but your goal is to find a bike that fits you and your frame. It's not your job to make your frame fit the bike frame. The second factor in buying a bike is how to maximize pedal power, and that has to do with your comfort, the bike setup, the bike fit, the bike accessories, and always drag, drag, drag—being aerodynamic to eliminate wind resistance.

If you can stretch your dollar or grab some additional ones, I urge you to consider a custom bike. Most stock bikes are built for men. A women's bike frame is a downsized men's bike. But men's anatomy and women's anatomy are quite different in almost every way. A women's complete custom bike can be purchased for $1,000–$2,000 depending on the components you choose. After riding most bikes on the market and struggling with the fit, I ordered a custom bike several years ago, and it has made a huge difference for my riding and my comfort. No longer am I stretched out over a top tube with brake levers that are too long and far apart for me to use effectively. Even though I'm a standard-size woman—five feet six inches and 135 pounds —stock bikes don't fit me well. I doubt they will fit you well either.

Used Bikes

Another option is to buy a used bike. There are many on the market to choose from. As with any used item, buyers should be cautious when purchasing a frame or frame set from a stranger. Find out before you buy a used bike everything you can about it—how old, how much use, what kind of use, how well cared for—the same questions you might ask when buying a used car. It's also important to know if the bike has been in an accident, as stress fractures on the frame usually are not obvious to the naked eye. Bikies are always looking to trade up, just as sports-car nuts do. You can get a good used bike for 50 to 75 percent of what a new one would cost. And if you don't know bikes really well, find somebody knowledgeable you can trust to help you make your selection.

Gearing

The different gearing arrangements pose another important decision to make. A certain elitism is built into the high-tech sport of triathlon, a snobbery that usually pertains to lightweight bikes with only a double chainring for the front chainwheel. (The front chainwheel is what your chain travels around on the front; the rear chainwheel is the round set of gears on the back that the chain rotates around.) I strongly recommend a triple chainwheel in the front—it's worth the weight to have enough gears to climb steep terrain easily for long periods of time. Examine the different gearing setups for road bikes and for touring bikes. Typical racing time trial bikes have front chainwheels with 53 teeth on the large one and 42 teeth on the small one. Touring bikes have front chainwheels of 52 teeth and 36 teeth respectively with the rear cogs of 14–34 teeth. In both, you will find the high gear combinations necessary for good speed on level roads or down hills. The touring bikes and cross bikes have more gears for pulling grades with heavier loads.

Wheels

One of the more important single components that can make a huge difference in performance is the wheels. Spend a little extra money to get good-quality lugs and light, strong rims. You will have to choose between alloy rims or composites with three or four spokes—or a combination of the two.

Bike Fit

To ride efficiently and comfortably, you must adapt your bicycle to your own needs. The bicycle–human body relationship is determined by certain important considerations you should know. According to Ironman champion Peter Reid in *Training Tips for Cyclists and Triathletes,* "When setting up a bike, you need to be aerodynamic to cut through the wind, but it is also important to be comfortable." Following are some basic guidelines for adjusting your bicycle to its human engine in a way that maximizes your comfort and minimizes your drag, your wind resistance:

Frame Geometry

Bicycle frames used to be measured by sizes, usually in inches such as 17, 19, 21, 23, 25, and so forth, or in the metric equivalents thereof. This represented the distance between the top of the seat tube and the middle of the bottom bracket. Today, frame geometry is more important than frame size. Do you want a triangle frame or a dropped top tube or a beam bike? To determine the type of geometry and frame size is an art, and the old methodology just isn't adequate today. I mentioned this in Chapter 4, but it bears repeating: If you go into a shop to get a bike fit and the saleswoman asks you to straddle the bike and measures your clearance, you know she is fitting it "the old way." Don't accept this. You want your body measured first, and there are computer software programs that can help you with this. Some bike shops charge to measure you, but it's worth every penny. You will get a printout showing what you need for bike frame measurements as well as components such as crank length and chainwheel sizes. The art, of course, is in the hands of the individual who measures you, because without precision at the start, the fit is compromised.

Saddle

It is very important to have the saddle fit your rear end rather than forcing your rear end to wear into the fit of the saddle. Likewise, the saddle position on the bike is important. There are basically three saddle-adjustment settings: angle, height, and forward/backward position. Just as I have repeatedly emphasized the individuality of everything—gear, training programs, nutrition, mental might—saddle position is also an individual preference. Some women prefer the nose of the saddle slightly tipped upward, I prefer mine downward, and still others like their saddle positioned parallel to the ground.

Saddle height is the next adjustment. There are many different ways to align the saddle over the crank, and making even slight changes can lead to differences in comfort and performance. To make adjustments, place your bike in a stable position with your heels on the pedals, barefoot. Choose a saddle height that you think is too low and pedal backward. Raise your seat height a quarter inch until your hips slide up and down as you complete a revolution of the crank. Once this sliding occurs, lower the seat position about a half inch. As Gale Bernhardt explains in *Training Plans for Multisport Athletes* (Velo Press, 2000), "A seat that is too high or too low can cause numbness in toes or genitals. Do not assume this is common; alleviate the problem."

Pedals

For every 2,000 miles you ride, you will rotate your pedals about a million times. For that many spins, pedal selection and adjustment are important. For adjustment, the ball of your foot should be directly over the pedal axle. There's no question that clipless pedals are the safest and lightest, but they are an upgrade to a standard bike. Yours will probably come with toe clips or cages. When you can, upgrade to clipless pedals. For pedals that come with a cage, you need the right size. They come in small, medium, and large; have the saleswoman help you with the sizing and fit.

Stem Height and Length

Your reach to the handlebars is the most critical part of your bike fit. If you go to a shop where they measure you, this will facilitate the process. The bottom line is that you are looking for the position that is most comfortable. Some women will be able to stretch out and lean down; others will find that position very uncomfortable.

Put your bike (or the one you are thinking of purchasing) on a trainer or have a friend hold you up. Start with the bars and seat level. Sit up straight (hands off the bars) with your shoulders back, chest out, and head held high. Rotate your feet so that the cranks are parallel to the ground. Now bend or hinge from your hips, without moving your neck or bending your back. Reach down to the handlebars, just until your hands are slightly above the brakes but not touching. Now gently rest your hands on the brakes (or bars if it has upright bars), putting very little pressure on them. You are looking for the position where you have some bend in your elbows, no pressure on the front of your saddle, and just a little on your hands. If you can move the bars up or down to achieve this position, then you're all set. If not, you will want to purchase a new stem that will position you in this manner. You want to be able to sit there comfortably for a half hour or so before you have to change your position.

In short, it doesn't matter what you look like; it matters what you feel like. If you need to sit up because of a back or neck injury, do it. If you're comfortable on your bike, you'll feel good when you get off it. If you get off with a sore back, you'll suffer in the running segment. The better you feel on your bike, the better you'll perform.

Handlebars

The type of handlebars you choose and their setup on the bike depend on your riding style and your anatomy. The new aerobars are trick and aerodynamic, but they also sacrifice bike-handling ability because they place your upper body weight on your forearms. For conventional drop bars, select the width that best corresponds to your shoulder width. Position the handlebars so that from a side view, the tops of the bars are parallel to the top tube.

Personal Choice

It will take you time to select a bike and almost that amount of time again to get the fit right on it. Spend the time. The joys of riding comfortably and efficiently depend on both. The bicycle, after all, is a machine that has been designed around you, the human engine. If the bicycle is compatibly matched to you, the energy expended in pedaling is efficiently converted into forward motion—the direction to the finish line.

The major factor in buying a bicycle is to decide what you want to do with it, both in triathlons and apart from them. Some women look for the best buy, and some have to buy the best. Bicycles certainly give you the chance to direct yourself toward either extreme. My advice is to decide what role the bicycle plays in your life and then buy the best one you can afford to suit that purpose. My vantage point is that I would rather pay more for a bike today and spend more time riding it because I love it. That is, there is a direct relationship between what you pay and what you get when purchasing a new bicycle. I prefer to pay more because in return I have a better chance of falling in love with it. If you love your bike, you're going to ride it more.

It will take time to select a bike and almost again that amount of time to get the fit right on it. Spend the time. The joys of riding comfortably and efficiently depend on both.

There have been many changes and improvements in bike technology in the past few decades. You can get a much better bike for the same money now than ever before, particularly where components are concerned. The changes are the result of sophistication in the use of materials, design, test results, technology, and the very nature of triathlon. Most triathlons are draft-illegal, which means that the time trial riding style prevails. Other triathlons are draft-legal and run on courses that are tighter with riders in packs, a factor that makes a criterium bike more advantageous. Take all of these factors into consideration when you start your bike shopping. But most of all, splurge on yourself: Every dollar you invest in that incredible two-wheeled machine can pay off in the romance of loving your bike.

Necessities

Helmet

This is the single most important item that you must purchase. In fact, one saved my life this year. After my bike accident (and after I awoke from the concussion), I looked at the two cracks and the skid marks that cut deeply into the side of my helmet, and I was unbelievably thankful, because the helmet cracked open and not my cranium.

Helmets must meet the safety requirements set the CPSC (Consumer Product Safety Commission). If the helmet meets their rigorous testing, a sticker is attached as a seal of approval. There are three other requirements to take into consideration: fit/comfort, ventilation, and weight. My unbreakable rule is that I won't ride with anyone who doesn't wear a helmet—either my cycling partners wear a helmet, or we don't ride together. It's a good rule.

Two Pumps

The first one to purchase is a frame pump, which you will carry with you on your bike because it's inevitable that you will have a flat. You can pump a bike tire to only about 60–80 psi (pounds per square inch) with a frame pump. Frame pumps are designed to get you home so you can use the second pump. Your second pump should be a high-pressure floor pump with a pressure gauge. You need a floor pump to fill your tires completely to the higher psi required for efficient riding. You can't push your thumb into the tire of a properly inflated tire, but check the tire sidewall for the number showing the manufacturer's recommended psi.

Tire Repair Accessories

Buy a bike accessory bag that will fit under your saddle, and put in the bag these minimum items: Cell phone or coins for a pay-telephone call, a speed lever, new tube (first flat), a patch kit (in case of a second flat), and your personal identification information, including an emergency phone number. You might also consider carrying a CO_2 canister (with adaptor), which can function as a quick alternative to hand pumping your tires after a flat.

Cage and Water Bottles

If your bike doesn't come with one, buy either a lightweight alloy or tough-plastic water bottle cage. There are also cages that attach behind your saddle or on your handlebars for ease and aerodynamics. I recommend carrying two water bottles for those hot days when you will really need them.

Reflectives

Any gear that provides reflective properties is a plus. Reflective clothing, equipment, patches, vests, reflectors attached to pedals, and tape for your helmet all light you up in a world where, as a cyclist, you appear obscure not only to cars but also to runners or other cyclists. Attach a rechargeable nickel-cadmium, battery-powered lamp with halogen bulbs to your frame if you are going to ride at night. The beams are bright enough that you can see the road very well.

Accessories

Aerobars

Standard "drop" handlebars work fine for triathlons. If you can upgrade, add a pair of aerodynamic bars with elbow pads. These are important for longer-distance triathlons such as international distance triathlons.

Bike Monitor

This is a hybrid monitoring device that consists of multiple functions such as a heart rate monitor, bike computer, and altimeter. Some examples of bike monitors are models manufactured by Specialized, Polar, and Cat Eye.

Clipless Pedals

Pedal systems such as Look, Speedplay, and SPD hook into a pair of bike shoes. Bike-shoe cleats typically come with the pedal system. Lightly clipping into your pedals with this system (shoe cleats and pedals) allows full use of the thigh (top and bottom) for the full rotation of the pedal stroke. They are called "clipless" because they don't have toe cages, known as toe clips.

Bike Computers (Cyclometers)

These tiny computers are a delight, because they give you informational feedback as you ride. A cyclometer attaches to your handlebars and works using magnetic impulses, which are transmitted to a computer chip, from a pick-up device mounted on the wheel. Bike computers measure pedal cadence, speed in miles per hour (or kilometers per hour), average speed, distance traveled (trip distance), total distance traveled to date, time of day, and duration of the ride. Some cyclometers can display several of these data functions simultaneously.

Unnecessary Accessories

Stock bikes are frequently equipped with unnecessary accessories. For example, kickstands are heavy and serve no useful purpose for a cyclist. You also don't need reflectors on your wheels; they slow you down, and if you are going to ride at night, you will wear reflective gear and use a front and rear light. Nor do you need valve stem caps, those little black plastic caps that screw onto the tire's valve stem. They slow you down when you want to fix a flat and serve no useful function.

Cyclewear

The cycling apparel industry has had an extremely colorful revolution since the hard-core days of bat-cave black. Getting cyclists to wear highly visible apparel for safety and colorful designs for fun and fashion, and to understand that shorts with leather-padded crotches cause more problems than they solve, has taken decades. Now the cycling consumer gets a choice of hot stuff with fit, form, and function.

Triathlon enthusiasts always have been diametric opposites—offer them something new that outperforms what they have been using, and they buy it by the thousands. Lucky for us triathletes, the cycling industry is finally offering cutting-edge, high-tech, high-performance products and apparel.

It's as important to dress in performance wear as it is to invest in performance components and equipment. Researchers have used wind-tunnel tests to measure performance differences among cyclists wearing different types of apparel and have demonstrated that wearing tight-fitting cycle wear can save the rider 10 percent or more in energy costs and time.

Shorts

The two concerns for all apparel are warmth and moisture control (the fabric's ability to wick dry). In the old days (maybe twenty years ago) riders wore black wool shorts with a chamois patch sewn into the crotch. Today, there are new fabrics and methods of construction that have changed all that.

In cold-weather riding, the new high-tech fabric blends are warmer and wick sweat better than do wools. In hot weather, Lycra stretch blends reflect the heat, allow perspiration to evaporate, dry quickly, and contour to the body more comfortably. A good design change is that chamois-lined pads have been replaced with softer and more hygienic polyester pads. Or, you can train comfortably without pads, in Lycra fitness or cross-training shorts.

Cycling shorts are worn without underpants, which are generally uncomfortable and annoying while bicycling. Therefore, because of the heat and sweat, cycling shorts must be washed after each ride. If you have problems with yeast infections, try different types of fabric blends in the inner lining. You will probably need several pairs of shorts if you ride frequently.

Shirts

Anything snug will do in this area. Some women prefer a Lycra bra-top with an overshirt that is removed once they are warmed up. However, if you crash and your shoulders aren't covered, you risk serious abrasions.

In the pre-triathlon era, women wore black wool jerseys (to match the color of bike grease) with pockets sewn onto the back. The term "bike jersey" comes from those olden days, when the shirts were made from wool jersey material. Today, like shorts, cycling jerseys are constructed from performance fabrics and are cut in fashionable styles.

In colder weather, multiple layers of apparel are recommended: A durable wind-jacket (preferably water resistant), over a long-sleeve performance-fabric turtleneck, over a short-sleeve shirt, over a performance-fabric tank will give you four layers, and that should be enough to keep you warm in most conditions. If you want more, add arm and leg warmers to your ensemble.

Companies that sell only women's activewear, such as Danskin and other fine manufacturers, are currently producing cross-training apparel. Cross-training apparel is designed for multifitness athletes who want to wear the same apparel for cycling, running, cross-country skiing, rock climbing, swimming, and other sports and is ideal for your tri-training needs.

As for those pockets sewn on the back of bike jerseys, most triathletes prefer to carry their extra stuff—food, sunscreen, tires—in fanny packs or under-the-seat accessory packs. It's easier to carry your gear in a fanny pack that can be taken off than to wear everything stuffed into pockets worn on your back.

Gloves

Cycling gloves are cut off at the knuckles for gripping power. They are designed to protect you from the road shock that is transferred to your hands through the handlebars and to protect your hands when you crash. However, I've always preferred to pad my handlebars, not my hands, with handlebar material like foam rubber and to avoid crashing. This means that I don't wear cycling gloves for rides under twenty miles unless I need them for warmth. It's your choice.

Socks, Hats, and Eyewear

If it's hot, I wear neither a hat under my helmet nor socks. If the weather turns cool, all of that changes. I hate to be cold, so I adopt the attitude that there's no cold weather, only warm clothing.

Investing in quality protective clothing is the key to never being cold. Wearing polypro socks (with plastic baggies over them if you need to) and bike booties over your shoes is usually enough to keep your feet warm. Placing a hat under your helmet may cause a problem with a good fit, but it does keep your head warm. Plastic-framed glasses will protect your eyes from both bugs and the elements, and ski masks or balaclava can further cover and warm your face.

Dress for the occasion: the temperature, the sun exposure, the rain (hopefully not snow), the fog, the wind speed, and the strenuousness of your ride. Dress for success, and be prepared to strip it off or pile it on as needed.

Running

I love the sport of running because of its simplicity. There are no elaborate facilities and no machinery to break down—just clothing and shoes, which together should cost around $100–$150. This includes top-of-the-line training shoes, which I discuss later along with some other accessories. You should, however, have a heart rate monitor, wear reflective tape or a vest that helps you be seen by cars at night, and carry identification with you whether you are swimming, cycling or running.

Running Gear

Shoes

Shoes, of course, are the runner's lifeline. Spend time at a specialty running shop to get a professional fit on your running shoes, and invest about thirty minutes to try on at least six models to find the right one. Trust your feet, not the sales pitch; they know best. Take your time in the store. A hasty choice will make your feet suffer. Manufacturers have specialized to such a degree

Sally Edwards co-founded Fleet Feet in 1976.

that you'll be able to find a shoe designed for the style of runner you are and for your specific biomechanics. If you're heavy, have narrow or wide feet or ankles, are hard on shoes, want lots of rear foot support, are a pronator, or need more cushion, don't despair. There's a running shoe out there for you.

When I first started selling athletic shoes in the retail chain I co-founded in 1976, Fleet Feet Sports, I ran into two problems: First, there were few styles specifically designed for women's feet, and second, the ones that were sold for women were smaller versions of the shoes made for men, with the word "lady" added before the name, such as the Nike "Lady Cortez." Today both these situations have changed. Manufacturers now recognize female athletes as women and use the word "woman" instead, and around 90 percent of shoe companies have taken to building women's shoes around the shape of a woman's foot, instead of just producing scaled-down versions of male-shaped ("lasted") shoes.

Running shoes are the single most important piece of equipment for a runner. If you have never run in a pair of real running shoes, go immediately to a specialty sports shop and take a pair for a test ride. They are so incredible, compared with cross-trainers or tennis shoes, that you won't leave the shop without them.

With new styles being released every six months and old styles being discontinued just as quickly, it is impossible to describe training shoes based on model or style. You no longer can find the right shoes and then keep purchasing them over the years—they will probably be discontinued before you wear out your first pair. Rather, to find the right shoe for you, look for one that provides shock absorption, stability, adequate flexibility, a last that matches your foot's shape, pronation support (for the way the foot rolls in after contact with the ground), and motion control. The biomechanics of your foot should match perfectly with the structural performance of your running shoe, and only a specialist who knows the current technology in performance footwear can help you with this. It's a good idea to cultivate the people at your local running store, since they can help you the most in finding the proper shoe for you. Buy your shoes from people who know running and running shoes.

Your basic choice is between racing flats (which weigh about 5 ounces) and running shoes (which are about 10–14 ounces). For now, select the heavier but more stable running shoes. Later, if you are so inclined, buy a pair of the racers—they are heavenly and make you feel almost barefoot when you run. If you have a wide foot, you might want to experiment with men's models, so keep in mind that an equivalently sized men's shoe will be 1½ sizes less than a women's shoe (for example, a women's 8 equals a men's 6½). Your new shoes don't generally require a break-in period; just lace them up, put on a pair of lace locks (plastic devices that prevent your laces from coming untied), and take off for an enjoyable few miles.

When you reach the half-life of your running shoes (at roughly 300 miles or 6 months, whichever comes first), purchase another pair but of an entirely different technology and style. Then alternate wearing the old pair with the new ones. A primary cause of running injuries is wearing the same shoes for every run. If you have a biomechanical weakness and you wear the same pair for every workout, you could fall prey to a cumulative injury effect.

Maintain your running shoes and don't use them for other sports; these are sport-specific footwear, not cross-training shoes. Occasionally check the wear points on your soles, and if you wear them out, especially in one place, either buy some patching goo from the running/triathlon store or get a new pair. The midsoles are probably shot anyway, although the outsole should last for a thousand miles unless you are a foot dragger.

Another word of advice from an old shoe dog: Buy the best pair you can afford. Choose value over price, because running shoes are an investment. It's cheaper to buy top-of-the-line running shoes than it is to pay for one visit to the doctor's office for a foot injury.

Sports Bras

When I first started running, there were no sports bras. Women either wore a Lycra swimsuit (interestingly, we still do today) or a support bra. Now many companies make sports bras, and no longer are bras uniformly white—they are designed with wild patterns and prints and can even be worn as outerwear.

Bras that are designed for athletics, rather than aesthetics, serve two primary purposes. First, sports bras prevent a variety of possible injuries to breast tissue: contusions, soreness or abrasions such as jogger's nipple (raw and/or bleeding nipples due to prolonged rubbing against a bra or shirt), or hematomas. Second, sports bras provide support to breast tissues from excessive movement. Large-breasted women in particular need to make sure their sports bra gives enough support and may need to wear two bras together. Pick one that is tighter and smaller and layer a slightly looser and larger one over it for better support.

Proper bra fit is key to preventing breast movement during vigorous activity. The bra should limit the movement in reference to the body, allowing the breasts to move only with the trunk rather than to bounce separately. Accordingly, athletic bras should provide you with the following benefits:

- Wide straps that are nonelastic and designed not to slip off the shoulders, such as the Y-back design
- Covered fasteners that do not cause abrasions
- A nonmetal underwire, such as a wide cloth band, that prevents the bra from riding up over the breasts
- Construction from absorptive, nonallergenic, and nonabrasive materials with little elasticity, such as the CoolMax fabrics
- Good upward support
- Limited motion of the breasts in relationship to the movement of the body
- Distribution of the weight of the breasts evenly over the rib cage and the back rather than the shoulders

Try on several different bra styles and test them by jumping up and down and by swinging your arms, both over your head and in running style. Also take a few deep breaths, as a bra should not interfere with breathing; a sports bra should be firm but not tight or restrictive to body motion.

Apparel

In her 1976 best-selling classic *Women's Running,* my friend Joan Ullyot wrote, "Apart from shoes, what you choose to wear is unimportant." At that time, most of us would have agreed with her, but her statement just doesn't hold in the twenty-first century. It's not that you have to dress for success, but rather that performance apparel can make a performance difference. Apparel that fits and is of the right fabric can prevent chafing, wick perspiration away from your body, maintain warmth, lower wind resistance, and prevent drag in the water and through the air. For any one of those features alone, it's worth it to be choosy. Cotton is not recommended for training apparel, since it retains water and thus keeps the moisture next to your skin, which can cause chafing and chills when it's cold.

Bottoms

You have a lot of choices. First, fitness, or "compression," shorts are made of stretch fabrics and are cut slightly longer than normal shorts, usually extending to just above the knee (which may prevent thigh chafing). Tights are full length, with stirrups, zippers, or neither, and are great for cold weather. Tricot nylon shorts, with liners cut to a woman's body shape, are lightweight (so light you feel you have nothing on) and durable. Briefs, or "butt huggers," might work for elite runners, but they leave nothing to the imagination and don't work for me.

Tops

The layered approach in apparel works for both its insulating properties and convenience. In cold weather, layering starts with a sports bra (always, for me, and I highly recommend you wear one), then continues with a performance-fabric short-sleeve top, a long-sleeve shirt, and a jacket or vest that is both warm and breaks the wind. All that remains is to add a few turtlenecks made of fabrics such as Dry Zone or polypropylene to your wardrobe, and you'll have your top covered.

Tri-Suits

These one- and two-piece outfits are a combination of a fitness short and a swimsuit top. They are sleek and true cross-training apparel, with the built-in advantage that when you wear them, you don't have to spend any time in the transition changing out of a swimsuit and into your biking or running apparel.

Outerwear

Remember the 20-degree rule—add 20 degrees (Fahrenheit) to the ambient temperature, and that's how hot it will be during your run. You should dress for the 20-degree rule, keeping in mind that hot-weather running requires more consideration than cold, because overheating is more immediately dangerous than cold-weather exposure. When it's hot, expose as much of your body as you can and wear light, loose-fitting tops. Don't tuck in your shirt, and do wear a visor or cap to shade your face. Also take care to drink lots of fluids during your workout, and run through sprinklers if possible.

Cold-weather running is easier, because you can add layers that trap the heat in. A stocking cap and gloves are standard fare. Wear polypro-type blended fabrics for warmth; they also have wicking properties that allow moisture to escape and warmth to stay in. To combat wet weather, wear waterproof fabrics such as Gore-Tex (which is also breathable). A run in the cold or in the rain can be as enjoyable as any other if you dress for success.

Socks

Whether to wear socks is a matter of personal preference. Some of my training partners never wear socks, and others wear blister-free socks that are double-layered on the bottom. Most runners wear socks for hygiene reasons, since it's easier to wash socks than shoes. Some people may get blisters without socks, some do with them, and some get them either way. It's up to you to test and find out how you're most comfortable.

Makeup

Don't bother with cosmetics before your run—you'll look worse afterward if you do. Skin-care products, though, are an exception. Vaseline can protect your hands and feet from chafing and blistering, and sunscreen is a must—apply it to all exposed areas. Take care of your skin; it is with you for a lifetime.

Triathlon Specialty Products

Specific triathlon specialty products have been created both for improvement of your performance through functional design and new materials and for fashion coordination. Everything from one-piece tri-suits to triathlon bicycles to triathlon wetsuits is now available, because such equipment can make a difference in your speed and training performance. Open-water swim goggles are another triathlon-driven product that can make an enormous difference in your comfort in the water—you can see clearly out of them in most directions. Indeed, the sport is inviting entrepreneurs to develop new and better products that will enhance our speed in multisport racing.

Another point that bears repeating here is to shop for your triathletic gear in specialty sports shops, especially your local tri-shop. Salespeople in discount, department, or hardware stores are not trained for the triathlete's specific needs. The sales staff at specialty stores are trained to sell bike, swim, and footwear gear. They will help you select the right equipment to meet your needs, your body size, and your budget. The running-shoe shop has a wide selection of top-quality brands, and bike shops can set up your bike properly, measure you for it, and provide repairs. Ask around to find out which businesses are best known for their service and expertise. In a good specialty store, you will find friendly people who understand athletes, because they are frequently athletes themselves.

TRIATHLON TRANSITIONS:
T1 AND T2

Transitions are unique to triathlons. They are a special place and time within a triathlon competition. Throughout this time, the race clock is running. Transition time can be well spent and efficient, though it may require a new set of tools and skills.

During the 2000 Sydney Olympics, the women's triathlon competition was, for most viewers, the supreme event of the entire Games. As we watched the women transition at the speed of light, it became clear that those who finished in front in the swim did not always leave T1, the swim-to-bike transition, in front. Rather, they were what triathletes call "out-transitioned." If you have ever been out-transitioned, it means you were slow getting through the transition, and that may be why you didn't finish ahead of your competition.

After my first Ironman competition in Hawaii in 1982, I returned home and vowed to write the first book on the sport to help others learn from my struggles. I hadn't found any resources for training or for racing or for how to transition efficiently. In that book, *Triathlon: A Triple Fitness Sport,* I introduced some new paradigms about cross-training and the benefits of triple fitness. At the time, triathlon was about merging three different fitness activities into one event, not about Olympic competitions and celebrity triathletes. I had to self-publish my inaugural book because no publisher then wanted to risk putting out a book on our infant sport. Later, I found an eager publisher, and *Triathlon* became its best-selling sports book, which shows that, like triathlons, personal and professional risks can pay off for all involved.

In that first book, in a category that came to include hundreds of titles on cross-training and triathlons over the next twenty-five years, I included a glossary of terms that became the underpinning language of triathlon. Two terms (on page 33) are applicable here:

> *Transition:* The time period in a triathlon race between the swim, bike, and run portions of the race.
> *Transition area:* The place where triathletes switch from one stage to another.

These definitions are as accurate today as they were decades ago. Triathlon then was considered an extreme sport, and as those of us who pioneered it set its course toward Olympic status, we laid the foundation for training methodologies.

The significance of transitioning is that it has two distinct aspects. The first is the transition activities you perform within the transition area. The second is the place called "the transition area" where these activities occur. There are ways to be more efficient and save energy and time by using both the transition activities as well as the transition area to your advantage.

The Transition Landscape

In the sport of triathlon, the early bird most often gets more than merely a worm. She also gets the prime spot in the transition area if she arrives early and it's an open-rack triathlon. Transition areas have two types of setups: open and designated racks. Some races require that you rack your bike in a designated area, which is usually determined by age, wave number, or your assigned race number. In an open-rack race, you can choose where to rack your bike.

Where you rack your bike can have substantial time advantages. In the open-rack system in which you have a choice, most triathletes choose to rack their bike closest to the transition area entry from the swim finish. Others prefer to rack their bike by the bike start. Find out in advance what the racking situation will be.

Few races today allow you to ride your bike in the transition area because of the severe congestion there. Transition areas can be dangerous; they are like a three-ring circus with multitudes of athletes milling around simultaneously.

Consider the normal scene of a triathlon in progress: Swimmers are running into the transition area, dodging cyclists in bike cleats who are jogging their bikes out of the area and who are encountering other cyclists running their bikes back into the area searching for their transition spot, as runners are leaving after the bike segment to start the run—and all the while, race volunteers are inside the area trying to help organize traffic flow. Then a bike rack collapses because there are more bikes racked than it was built for, or a triathlete can't find her transition place, or someone is cold or injured and in need of aid. In short, the scene becomes total bedlam. That's the nature of the transition area.

How do you avoid getting caught up in this situation? You can't. All you can do is be polite, avoid the congestion, laugh at the chaos, and smile inside, because through it all, it's fun. It's like being a kid again and you were just given permission to go play at your favorite childhood activities—swimming, cycling, and running.

Finding your landmarks or counting bike racks is one way of saving time and headaches when you make a decision on where to rack your bike. As Joel Friel writes in *The Triathlete's Training Bible,* "Acquaint yourself with landmarks for your rack such as its position relative to trees, light poles, pavement marking, signs or other permanent markers." I like to use the rack-counting method to keep track of my bike in a transition area. I walk to the entrance to T1 and then walk back to where my bike is, counting the number of rows and then the number of racks in my row to the exact position of my bike transition spot. This position might be 5 rows by 3 racks on the left. Next, I go to the finish of the bike leg and follow the same procedure of counting bike racks so that I can find my towel and gear that are positioned at my transition place for T2. This second rack counting might be 10 bike rows by 5 bike racks. I memorize the two numbers—5 by 3 for T1 and 10 by 5 for T2. As you become more fatigued during the race and confusion sets in, losing the location of your transition area can cause both frustration and delays.

Recently, one of my training partners, Estelle Gray, owner of Seattle's premier cycling retail store, R&E Cycles, was racing at a new venue. She followed her pre-race ritual of counting bike racks and memorizing the numbers and landmarks. After the swim she couldn't find her bike, wasting five minutes and hundreds of calories of emotional energy in the process. At the last minute, race management had changed the location of the entrance to the transition area. With 2,500 bikes and about three acres of transition area, she was lost. It was a serendipitous time for me, though: Estelle decided that continuing her race was pointless because of the lost time and instead joined me as the sweep cyclist. As we rode up next to the last rider on the bike course after the first mile, she casually said to the woman, "How would you like to make your bike go faster?" The woman grinned in agreement. Estelle, the bike aficionado that she is, said "shift gears," and with the ease of lower gears and higher pedal cadence, the two left me behind in a heartbeat.

The Eight Stages of a Triathlon

Most people think of a triathlon as a combination of three events. It's that—but more. A triathlon begins with the time your swim wave starts, continues with your bike segment, and ends when you cross under the finish banner at the end of the run. But the triathlon includes eight different events to prepare for, and two of them are your transitions. Transition time may be the shortest part of the eight events, but the time adds up, so saving a few seconds in each of the events can add up to minutes and, for some, even hours. These are the eight parts of a triathlon, and each has its own set of skills for you to master:

1. Start of the swim
2. Finish of the swim
3. T1
4. Start of the bike
5. Finish of the bike
6. T2
7. Start of the run
8. Finish of the triathlon

Training—mentally and physically—for each of these eight segments is what this book is about, and this outline helps you see the big picture: The eight legs of a triathlon give you a different vantage point from thinking of it as just a swim-bike-run event. Practice each T. Train for each T. And most of all, while you're in a T, make the most of it.

Transition Efficiency

Recently, I was stuck in traffic with my car radio tuned to Dr. Laura Schlessinger, the relationship expert, who was holding forth on one of her favorite topics—the stupid things people do to botch up a relationship. The same thing can happen in transition activities to botch up a good race, and just as Dr. Laura makes me laugh and think, so also do the mistakes we make during our transition activities.

The goal for transition activities is to get in and out of each of the two transition areas as quickly and efficiently as possible. Because race time includes your transition times, the faster you can get through your transitions, the faster your overall finish time.

As I listened to Dr. Laura lecture on our blunders in relationships, I thought about the potential blunders that can trip us up in our transitions. I've mentioned many of these throughout this book, but it's an apt time for review. Here are my top eight pointers for avoiding those blunders; many of them are accompanied by anecdotes that clearly drive the point home:

1. Getting to the Race Early

Recently, I was inducted into the Triathlon Hall of Fame, an event held in conjunction with one of the sports national championships. I invited several training buddies to join me for the celebration and challenged them the day before to enter a low-key event called the "Splash and Dash" for the sole purpose of having fun. They asked when to meet in the transition area, and I said I needed a mere thirty minutes to set up my transition area. Clearly, after over two hundred triathlon competitions, I still have a few lessons to learn, because it took longer than thirty minutes to get my gear set up.

The race was held in the ocean north of San Diego. The starters announced two important safety conditions, but we were still finding our transition spot and setting up our gear and missed the announcement. The two announcements were that there was a serious rip tide at the finish of the swim, and that the ocean currents were moving swiftly parallel to the shore and pushing swimmers into the pilings of the pier. Sure enough, we experienced the terror of both as we splashed and dashed into them, but both could have been avoided if we had arrived at the transition area at least an hour in advance.

2. Less is More

The less gear you can bring into the transition area and the fewer clothes you can wear, the faster and easier your transition can become. Use a check-list of essential gear (see Chapter 9) and keep your needs to a bare minimum. Every item of apparel you add during transition costs time in getting it on, especially when you're wet from the swim or tired from the cumulative fatigue of the bike. At the triathlon camps Danskin sponsors, we have timed how long it takes to put on socks before running shoes and pull on bike gloves before the ride. Both activities require about 20–45 seconds each, which can add precious time allocated for clothes you may not find necessary for your performance.

If you believe both of these or other items are essential, practice putting them on or using them under similar conditions as you will experience at a triathlon race. Timing yourself doing this can help you to decide whether they are truly needed. One thing you can be sure of, veteran triathletes have less stuff in their transition area than newbies do.

3. Buckets and Balloons

Finding your transition spot in a race of several thousand can be a difficult challenge. After you leave T1, the swim-to-bike transition, you have little to return to but a towel, your running gear, your cap and goggles, and your gear bag. Upon your return, the transition area looks entirely different, because you enter from a different direction and must find your transition spot. Some triathletes use markers such as helium-filled balloons, which they attach to the bike racks. This also makes the transition area look more like a playground than acres of parked bikes. Buckets also are used by some triathletes in transition to dip their feet in to remove grit and sand that collects after they leave the swim and before they mount their bike. I caution against using buckets because they create congestion and an obstacle. The transition area is a busy place, with athletes moving quickly and often somewhat recklessly. Rather than bringing a water bucket or pan, I'd recommend an extra water bottle that you can use to wash your feet and an extra towel to rub them dry.

4. She Who Enjoys the Event Wins

My fifty-four-year-old friend Lyn Cranmer, now from Bakersfield, California, a multitime Danskin and Ironman finisher, won't leave the transition area without reapplying her lipstick. At first, this nod to beauty seems whimsical and vain, but for her, it is important and therefore worth the investment of time and energy. She gives the competition an extra few seconds, but it doesn't matter to her. Lyn is not a pro, and she has always raced for the joy of being in the event. Hence, the choice of looking good is more important to her than her final finish time.

The same can be true about the outfit you select to wear during the triathlon. Pros swim, bike, and run in the same item of clothing without adding or removing apparel. If triathlons are more for fun than for bragging rights, then there is no question but that looking good reigns supreme over fast transition times. Bring on the fashion groups—it may be more important to look good than to go fast.

5. Pigging Out

I volunteer to finish last as the "sweep athlete" in most triathlons that I compete in today. I get paid to do so by the Danskin company, which prefers that a pro rather than a first-timer be the final finisher. I prefer being the last to finish: It's the best place in the race for one reason—the vantage point of being behind tens of thousands of women competing in their first triathlon. As the last woman out of the water, off the bike, and finishing the run, I get to see things that others can't even imagine. One of those is the "party" that many women have in the transition area. I see leftover cans of pop, pieces of chocolate cake, cookies, ice cream, and more that have been devoured as many of the gals refuel while they are transitioning. If you want to pig out in the transition areas, go to it. But I'll tell you, those who finish in front refuel during the race; they eat on the bike and on the run, not in the transition area.

6. Stress Makes Us Stupid

Dozens of times I have watched women leave the transition area on the run wearing their bike helmets, forgetting their race numbers, and leaving their hat or sunglasses behind. That is because when we enter the stress zones, it is nearly impossible to think clearly. Stress is our perception of emotional strain. Because of the pressure to transition fast, because of the effects of physical fatigue and high heart rates going into and out of transition areas, our brains get foggy. To resolve this phenomenon if it occurs for you, calm the mind and cool the heart. When you are in the transition area, breathe deeply, relax, take a drink of water, and stay focused on the activities required there— gear, apparel, and equipment changes. Taking a few extra seconds in transition to remain coolheaded is worth it if it saves you minutes during the next leg. My friend Kathy Kent, the president of Heart Zones Cycling, is proud of her quick transitions. She likes to chew gum on the run because she believes it keeps her mouth wet. She takes the time during her transition setup and during her T2 to grab a piece of gum because it helps her to run faster. If it works for you, then do it.

7. Stripping Off the Wetsuit

The first time I met a stripper was at Ironman Canada where volunteers were assigned the task of pulling off our wetsuits after the 2.4-mile swim. It probably gained me only five to ten seconds in an eleven-hour race, but it was helpful and I appreciated the consideration. It also was worth it because my hands were too cold to strip off my suit with any grace.

In most races, though, removing a wetsuit if you wear one is your responsibility. It sometimes helps to coat your calves and ankles lightly with something slippery that doesn't degrade the neoprene in the suit (Pam or Runner's Lube will work), and put some lubricant on your neck and other body areas where abrasions might occur. The benefits of wearing a wetsuit far outweigh not using one because it keeps you warm and buoyant during the swim leg. If your wetsuit fits well, you can shave minutes off your swim time. Using a wetsuit changes your body position in the water. You swim faster because your body position is higher in the water and that means less drag. But if you're like one triathlete I met in the water who was struggling with her wetsuit, wearing it backward will definitely slow you down (note: most wetsuits zip in the back).

8. Keep It Simple, Stupid

Throughout this book, I've given you some simple tricks that help keep transitions simple. First, remember that your transition space is very small, no larger than ten to twelve square feet, so you don't have much room for gear. For example, take all your swim gear with you to use in the swim; there should be no swim stuff left behind except for your towel, which is on the ground. Pump up your tires after you remove your bike from your car, not in the transition area; leave your bike floor pump and bike tools in your car.

Also, carry the least amount of repair gear you can in your bike saddlebag and have your bike checked before the race; don't wait until race morning. Don't do anything new in the race that you haven't tried in training. Hydrate in advance of the race, especially if the race is longer than an hour, and nibble on something if you are in one of the last wave starts—which may be as much as two hours after the first wave hits the water. Get your gear organized the night before and pack it so that all you have to do on race morning is roll out the door—hotel or home—with a bike and gear bag. Most of all, do things the smart way: Keep it simple.

10. The Winner Is Whoever Makes the Fewest Mistakes

A few years ago, in Austin, Texas, Danskin, I was again serving as the sweep triathlete, riding with a water-logged gal who was in an early swim wave but whose swimming skills needed major improvement. We had been biking for about thirty minutes at ten miles per hour, her fastest speed, when a motorcycle cop rode up beside me to say there was a triathlete behind us. Astonished, I did a careful U-turn on the course (closed to traffic) to discover a frustrated woman indeed riding behind us. As we rode along, I asked how she got herself in the situation of being probably twenty minutes behind the second-to-last triathlete. She described her experience of exhaustion and panic: She had lost her helmet in T1 and had to run back to her car to get a spare, which cost her about forty minutes. Ironically, she was an Air Force officer responsible for logistics. I wondered how this specialist in organization and execution could now be dead last in the triathlon, especially with her background in logistics.

Her experience serves as a paramount example of how planning and logistics are at the heart of triathlon events. Be organized. Follow the Girl Scout creed known as "be prepared," and you won't be swimming, biking, or running with me in your next triathlon as the final finisher.

The All-Important Transition-Area Setup

When you arrive at the race, park your car and get your apparel and gear organized, remembering the tip that less is more. As you walk toward the transition area, you will probably see long lines of participants waiting for their turn at the portable toilets, a common sight because using the facilities before the race is more comfortable and saves time during the race. As you near the transition area, body markers usually meet you; these individuals with black felt pens write your race number in large print on various highly visible locations on your body.

Spectators are not allowed in the transition area, so say goodbye for a few minutes as you roll your bike into the transition area and decide where to rack it (whether it's open or designated racking.) After selecting your transition spot, place your bike on the bike rack and start your setup by checking the following:

- Your water bottle is full of fluid.
- You are in the proper gear when you first mount the bike based on the terrain.
- Make one final safety inspection: brakes, tires, quick releases, and more.
- Make sure your race number is affixed to your bike frame.

Next, place a small towel parallel to your back wheel. Empty your gear bag of its contents, and store your bag next to your front wheel. Place all of your gear items on the towel in the sequence in which you will use them. (Use the checklist provided in Chapter 9.) Double-check that everything is organized and that you have been thorough in setting up your transition area. Make one last check that your race number is in the transition area—affixing it to a race belt may save as much as fifteen seconds. If the race is using "chip timing," affix the computer chip using the Velcro attachment system.

Do your location analysis next: Where is your bike racked in relation to the finish of the swim, the start of the bike segment, and the end of it. Count bike racks, find landmarks, and perhaps attach your marker balloon or your brightly colored towel so that you can easily find your bike and transition gear. Walk the route that will take you into the swim area, out of it onto the bike, and off the bike and out on the run—all transition-area navigational requirements that must be completed efficiently even though you're fatigued and in a congested situation.

Your transition is set up. You're done. It's time for the triathlon race to begin.

Next, grab all of your swim gear (goggles, swim cap, and [optional] wetsuit) and enjoy a few moments before the start of the race meeting new friends, taking a quiet moment, using the facilities, hydrating, doing some stretching and warmup activities, reviewing your strategy, and mentally doing what you can do to focus your energy on the upcoming eight events that are the pieces of a triathlon. Take one last look at your transition area as the announcer calls you to the starting line, and relax: You have it in order. Head to the starting line with the knowledge that, as we say in the Danskin, *the woman who starts the race is not the same as the woman who finishes.*

TEAM SURVIVOR

After a diagnosis of cancer, one doesn't always feel like going for a run or heading out for the gym. The motivation to exercise following a cancer diagnosis shifts from prevention to survival. Women do not always know how to begin their recovery from cancer and begin or continue an exercise program. Women cancer survivors can get this kind of help through group exercise programs offered through Team Survivor. Team Survivor promotes fitness by giving cancer survivors the support, skills, and knowledge needed to reach and maintain their health and fitness goals. Women who are actively undergoing chemotherapy or radiation treatment, recovering from surgery, affected by advanced disease, or dealing with survivorship issues can benefit from the Team Survivor programs. General physical health is promoted through weekly monitored exercise sessions, walking programs, and educational forums on health, exercise, cancer (such as lymphedema, nutrition, alternative health, and stress management).

Exercise can have multiple health benefits for cancer patients:

- Improved healing and recovery from surgery
- Decreased lymphedema
- Higher energy levels, less fatigue
- Weight loss/weight gain

• Decreased nausea
• Less pain
• Improved body and self-image
• Decreased anxiety
• Improved social interactions
• Better sense of control
• Less depression, improved mood
• Better sleep patterns

Cancer patients may consider continuing their regular workout programs throughout cancer treatment. Retaining as much of your lifestyle as you can, such as your exercise program, can be a powerful coping tool. Some patients may need to modify their exercise regimen, but it is not necessary to "just walk." Regardless of your exercise mode, you may need to change the intensity level.

Chemotherapy

Chemotherapy often lowers blood counts, which may decrease oxygen delivery throughout the body. Lisa Talbott, M.P.H. and one of America's experts on cancer and exercise, recommends keeping heart rates low, approximately 65 percent of max HR (zone 2) to reduce early onset of fatigue during exercise. A slower pace will not only allow for longer workouts but will also improve daily energy levels. A good way to start an exercise routine without increasing fatigue is to do shorter bouts of exercise twice a day. Rather than aiming for a twenty- or thirty-minute walk, try walking just ten minutes two or three times a day. These shorter sessions will begin to increase your endurance without depleting your energy reserves. Exercise for cancer patients is most effective when approached on a more holistic level. Yoga, for example, is the perfect complement to aerobic, energy-producing exercise such as walking. Yoga increases muscle flexibility and strength and is highly meditative. Many hospitals, cancer wellness centers, and fitness facilities are now offering yoga and other exercise and movement classes specifically for cancer survivors.

Team Survivor and the Danskin

Many women facing a diagnosis of cancer need to prove to themselves and others that they are "okay." Most rethink the purpose, goals, and direction of their lives and make a commitment to experiencing and accomplishing things for which they have either never had time or never before thought possible. A key program of Team Survivor is preparing women to complete their first triathlon through the Danskin Women's Triathlon Series. Such fitness challenges encourage tremendous personal growth as the women succeed at new and difficult experiences. Many Team Survivor participants are in active treatment for their cancer during their first Danskin triathlon race, then return each year to take on another Danskin. They cite the Danskin experience as a key factor in their ongoing, lifelong recovery and growth process.

Team Survivor provides women cancer survivors with a fun, positive, and inspiring experience of physical activity. Succeeding at a regular exercise program and setting a goal such as completing a triathlon are major ways to improve body image and self-esteem and cement the commitment to a healthy lifestyle. When women feel they have control of their bodies during and after cancer treatment, they are empowered to return to work or school and take on new physical or emotional challenges.

The true benefit of the Team Survivor program is best expressed in the stories of some women who have participated in it:

Belinda

The first time I was diagnosed with breast cancer was in 1989. I had a lumpectomy on my right breast. The lymph nodes that were removed were negative. I went through radiation and chemotherapy. I was teaching first grade at the time and I continued working during my therapy. The doctors thought they had caught my tumor in time. In 1994 I had a recurrence of the cancer. It had spread to my liver and bones. The doctor told me that the cancer was terminal and that I had one or two years to live. We began aggressive treatment. I developed congestive heart failure and could not have a planned stem cell transplant. I was put on Tamoxifen when the chemotherapy failed. My heart ejection fraction was severely reduced at 30 percent, and I was told this would not get better. . . . My husband said that if I could exercise and strengthen my heart, maybe I would live long enough for there to be a new treatment. I started going on walks with my neighbor Tina and her dog. At first it took me forty-five minutes to walk a block. A few months later I could walk a mile in forty-five minutes. One day, while looking through my mail, I found an invitation for cancer survivors. A few weeks later I went to a meeting of Team Survivor. The group was watching a video of a triathlon they had completed. I was amazed. I remarked that there was no way I could do anything like that. A lady standing next to me asked me, "Why not?" I told her I didn't have a bike. She said, "So get one." I said I had not ridden since high school. She said, "So start riding." I said I couldn't swim well enough. She said, "Practice." I said I couldn't run. This lovely lady, Bonnie Wegner, said, "Walk." I finished my first triathlon on August 19, 1996. I had just gone into remission. I finished two more triathlons in 1997 and 1998. They have been wonderful experiences for me. I have a bike, a cool helmet, an Ironman wetsuit, and cross-training shoes. Tamoxifen has been replaced with Anastrazole. I am still battling cancer ... I will always have to fight. Every day I thank God for my life. I'm stage IV and still here. Who knew?

Karen

The first few hours after I learned that I had been diagnosed with breast cancer were a jumble of phone calls, confusion, and emotion. One of the first clear and constructive thoughts I had during that time, however, was that continuing my running routine was likely to be a big help in coping with whatever was ahead. During the next few weeks of uncertainty and fear, I found that I felt happy, almost giddy, when I went out for a run. My running represented a part of my life that I could control. No matter what I was to learn about my prognosis over the coming weeks, there would still be a part of my life that I could define and manage strictly for myself. As I went through the treatment course, my energy level dropped significantly, and the bulk of my running shifted to walking. Despite a good prognosis, I was emotionally fragile, and I experienced every feeling very deeply. Knowing that my walks gave me uninterrupted time for introspection made this barrage of feelings much less intimidating. A month after my treatment was complete, I set out with my husband Andy for one of our favorite runs, on a trail near the Connecticut River and the Dartmouth College campus. It was the longest run I had taken since my diagnosis, and I surprised myself a bit with my stamina. During the last half mile, a steep and rocky hill, I recognized a type of fatigue different from what I had been experiencing over the previous few months. "This fatigue isn't about the cancer," I told myself. "This fatigue is about being an athlete and training and not hanging back from this hill." I gave a quiet "thank you" to the runner in me, recognizing how important she had been as I struggled with the feelings surrounding my cancer and looking forward to an ongoing recovery process where I continued to feel strong and in control of my body and my health.

Carla

Six weeks after my bilateral mastectomy and reconstruction, I suffered a triple ankle fracture. It was like getting up after one truck hit me, only to be hit by another. Perhaps that's what it took to get my attention, to make me stop and think about where my life was going and how I had not been taking care of myself. I had been a slender, active teenager and continued to exercise and enjoy the outdoors into my thirties. But a sedentary lifestyle and a typical, too-fat American diet had taken over. Early menopause had brought extra pounds and lethargy. Now I had a real wake-up call. After recovering from the ankle repair surgery, I began to walk in my neighborhood. I found out about a water exercise program for cancer survivors. There I found not just physical recovery but also camaraderie with other survivors. In 1995, I was proud to walk the 5K portion of the Austin Danskin Triathlon with Team Survivor. My teammates challenged and inspired me. Along with the physical recovery came emotional healing, too. I conquered a great deal of fear and self-doubt, largely with the support of my training partners and the Team Survivor coaches, but also from friends and family. I now exercise four or five times a week, with my husband, a longtime friend, and my Team Survivor buddies. People I have not seen in several years say I look younger. That may be mainly flattery, but I do know I look and feel much healthier than I did seven years ago!

Kathy

As I was growing up, exercise had always been a part of my life. I played competitive tennis and softball and also enjoyed biking, swimming, golfing, and skiing. In college, I took up canoeing and tried cross-country skiing. Little did I realize that a decade later, this exercise would help me cope and survive with life. In June 1989 my worst fear had come to be: I had cancer and would have to undergo chemotherapy. I thought my life was over, because at that time, I had never known anyone who had survived chemotherapy, let alone exercised while on chemo. This was a devastating thought, but my oncologist told me that I would still be able to live a normal life though I might have to slow down. I was able to continue to exercise daily, work full-time, and play softball and tennis. Five years later, I had a heartbreaking recurrence and was told I would benefit from a bone marrow transplant. They told me I would probably be off work for six to eight months and would have to take it very easy. I was able to return to work within six weeks after the transplant—this I attributed to being in a somewhat good physical condition. I was happy to be on the road to recovery, but I continued to coddle myself because I was afraid to do anything too strenuous. Seven months after the transplant, I had heard about a women's triathlon where they had a program for women cancer survivors. I decided this would help me to start my "new life" and joined the program, Team Survivor. I set a goal to try to do the 3.1-mile run without stopping; this alone would be a major accomplishment. Because I had not swum or biked in years, I decided to forgo the swimming and biking and to concentrate on the run. On race day, I decided to do the swim accompanied by my coach. Although I hadn't trained for this part of the race, I just felt so empowered by all the women and support I was feeling that I went for it. Much to my amazement, I finished the swim

Sally Edwards as the "final finisher" at one of her 80 Danskin finishes.

and ran the entire 3.1 miles without stopping or walking. Thus began my "new life" and my road to recovery. Through exercise, the support of friends, family, the medical community, and God, I was able to accomplish something beyond my wildest dreams. The best part was that I was still intact after that first triathlon, and I am alive today to tell the story. With help, I was able to go beyond my limits. With this help, I am able to *survive*.

Jeanne

You don't have to be an athlete to enjoy exercise as part of your lifestyle. And you are never too old to begin. I began doing aerobics at age fifty-three. I was diagnosed with breast cancer in the summer of 1989, and immediately after surgery I continued aerobics in a limited way during the six weeks of radiation. Then I left on a planned trip to Papua New Guinea for four weeks of rather active travel. I felt great. In 1995 a member of Team Survivor Northwest introduced me to some of their activities. . . . I began cycling and learning bike care and attended Wednesday evening workouts. In 1997, Team Survivor introduced me to snowshoeing. . . . I love the great exercise it provides and the beauty of the surroundings. In 1998 I began to train for the Danskin Women's Triathlon. Team Survivor provided us with a coach, training activities, schedules, and support. It was a dark, rainy morning as I took off on the half-mile swim. It was as difficult as I expected, but I came out of the water to cheers and actually found the twelve-mile bike ride to be fun. Our ages were written on the back of our calves, and as the younger, stronger riders passed me and read the figure "68," they cheered me on. As I crossed the finish line with three other Team Survivor members, our arms on each other's shoulders, it was a great moment. I placed first in my age group (65–69), but I must confess that I don't believe I had much competition. The important thing was that I finished *and* I felt great afterward—that was my goal. The friends I have made through exercising have been a wonderful plus, and have added much to my life in ways other than exercise, too.

Sharon

First, I must admit I am a competitive, determined, and motivated person. I was the top-ranked female triathlete in the 40–44 age group in the South/ Midwest region for the 1998 season. I was on top of the world, in peak shape, and leading a healthier life than I ever had. Six days later I was diagnosed with breast cancer. I had a lumpectomy with sentinel node biopsy surgery. The next weekend, I was riding my bike and 1 week later doing a track workout. I just pushed myself to do what I could. I found I could still do a lot. I would leave radiation and go swimming or running. I didn't stop; I just slowed down. I found I could still place in my age division although I was slower. Two and a half weeks into radiation treatment, I won my age division at a challenging duathlon known for its harsh weather conditions. Then two weeks following the completion of radiation, I did a Race for the Cure 5K run. I was the first survivor across the finish line and second in my age division. It helped ease some of the anger I had about getting the disease. By far the most comprehensive treatment I have found since my diagnosis has been Team Survivor Austin. As I already had a fairly high-intensity training program, I joined Team Survivor for the emotional support and companionship found with the other women cancer survivors interested in fitness and health. The team helps me maintain a healthy balance in my life and makes each time I train and race count more. My present goal is to train and race as a visible cancer survivor to let other women cancer survivors know anything is possible. When Lance Armstrong, a testicular cancer survivor, won the 1999 Tour de France, he said it all: "If you ever get a second chance in life, you've got to go all the way."

How to Contact Team Survivor

Team Survivor is a national nonprofit organization that provides free exercise, health education, and support programs for women affected by cancer. To join a Team Survivor program in your area, contact Team Survivor USA at www.teamsurvivor.org. Most Team Survivor programs are supported by volunteer efforts. What better way to stay in shape than to volunteer for a fitness organization like Team Survivor? You do not need to be a cancer survivor to volunteer for these programs.

CAMP DANSKIN

Camp Danskin Is for Fun

Camp Danskin is either a weekend-long or one-day triathlon training camp for fun and fitness. Our coaches teach you new skills both in the classroom and during group workouts. Creatively designed, the workouts include running, road biking, and swimming in either lakes or pools. The emphasis is on having a good time, meeting other women new to triathlon, and applying the latest training techniques and methods.

Camp Danskin Is for Everyone

Camp Danskin is designed for women of all ages and abilities. The workouts accommodate a variety of fitness abilities and experience. Whether you are a first-timer or an accomplished racer, you'll learn skills and techniques suited to your abilities and desires.

You'll leave this weekend with personalized coaching and the tools to create an individualized training program that nearly guarantees you will improve your triathlon experience. Camp locations vary year to year, but the locations are chosen for their scenic beauty and peacefulness. Meals are generous and nutritious.

For more information, contact
Camp Danskin
2636 Fulton Avenue, #100
Sacramento, CA 95821
www.Heartzones.com
E-mail: staff@heartzone.com

About the Camp Director

Jazz Scheingraber, the co-founder and director of Camp Danskin, is a collegiate All-American, professional coach, and international competitor in cross-country skiing. Jazz is an adventure athlete and placed third in ESPN's 1996 Survival of the Fittest, and she has completed numerous Eco-Challenge races. She's the Site Manager for the Danskin Women's Triathlon Series and is truly dedicated to seeing thousands of women get where they want to go: across the finish line at a Danskin Triathlon.

Jazz Scheingraber, head coach and director of Camp Danskin.

DANSKIN MENTOR-
MENTEE PROGRAM

Whether you are a first-time triathlete with questions about the sport or an experienced athlete who hopes to share your knowledge and enthusiasm about triathlon with a novice, the free Danskin Mentor-Mentee program could be for you.

This grassroots volunteer program is designed to match experienced athlete mentors with first-timer "mentees" in an effort to enhance the triathlon experience for all involved.

Through volunteer efforts, we've made training for your Danskin even more fun. The head mentor for the Mentor-Mentee program keeps the members informed about workout opportunities and matches mentors with mentees geographically through zip code. What a difference one phone call or e-mail can make for the first-timer!

Our Danskin Mentor-Mentee program is a short-term relationship between two participants or past participants of the Danskin. In such a relationship, the experienced participant provides help, support, and guidance to the first-time participant.

To All the Mentors

As a volunteer mentor you could

- Improve mentee's overall knowledge of the sport of triathlon
- Suggest ways for mentees to develop necessary skills for a specific racecourse
- Meet for workouts in pursuit of training for similar goals

Your best work is in the area of personal experience. Mentees don't expect you to be completely versed in triathlon lore (though some of you are), and they don't expect you to be in perfect condition (though some of you are), so be aware that mentees seek your opinions and suggestions. You have raced at this location, organized equipment, and received that finisher's medal at least once. You have the experience first-timers don't have today but will soon.

To All the Mentees

As a mentee you could

- Have the real-world experience of another Danskin triathlete at your fingertips
- Find scheduled workouts that get you out the door
- Share a laugh and smile over the sheer physical fun of fitness

For mentors, you will be the open-minded, enthusiastic, willing-to-try-anything-once, happy campers of this relationship equation. Mentors don't expect you to have made a lifelong commitment to fitness (though some of you have) or have a deep-rooted desire to be a professional triathlete (yet). Mentors are there to listen and feed back to you any tips or tricks they think you can use. You have lots of courage, and we all admire and respect you for it. After all, only you will be getting your body over that finish line.

If you are interested in joining the Danskin Mentor-Mentee program as a mentor, mentee, or even an Area Coordinator, contact us. Go to www.mentormentee.org for information on the program in your area, or send your name, address, phone number, and e-mail to Attn: Rebecca Yao, National Coordinator, 1075 Bellevue Way NE PMB 300, Bellevue WA 98004.

BUYING A NEW
HEART RATE MONITOR

There are a lot of choices today if you are in the market for a new heart rate monitor (HRM). With over 100 different models of HRMs to choose from made by dozens of OEMs (original equipment manufacturers), you the consumer have the opportunity to get the best. All you need to do is match the three factors: how much money you have budgeted, what features you want, and what your needs are. With this information, you can make the right choice the first time.

Before you buy a monitor (or an upgrade if you already have one) you must decide which manufacturer and model. First, take this simple "HRM buyer's test." The results will narrow your choices and increase the chance that the one you select has enough heartpower and horsepower for your needs.

HRM Buyer's Test: Five Questions to Making a Decision
DECISION 1.
There are three main features in HRMs. Which feature is most important to me?
Today, HRMs come in three classes: continuous-read monitors, zone-programmable monitors, and downloadable monitors. Here's a description of each type. Read before you select which feature best fits your pocketbook and needs.

- Continuous-read monitors. These are the simplest available and the least expensive. They are easy to recognize because they have no buttons. The only data you receive is heart rate in beats per minute. The numbers are big and easy to read. They are extremely durable and easy to operate. They are quite simply a no-brainer. They're my favorite model for swimming because they're easily readable with my goggles on. Ideal for swimmers, aerobicizers, walkers, and beginners of all types. They range in price from $50 to $75.

- Heart zone programmable monitors. Also called simply zone monitors, these HRMs are for the intermediate user. They allow you to program some features into the monitor such as recovery heart rate time, countdown timers, heart zones, and time in-above-below your heart zone. They are mid-priced and run in the $75–$150 range.

- Downloadable monitors. For the dedicated consumer who loves numbers, these HRMs (also called memory monitors) are for those who want to do extensive analysis of the data. HRMs are like minicomputers in that they use integrated circuits, and these models have a type of downloadable memory. The monitor stores the data—beats per minute and sometimes time—for later recall. With some models you can manually recall the data, and with others you can download data into a computer. Price range is $150–$300 for the monitor. Software and download boxes are often accessory items.

DECISION 2.

Are you willing to make the commitment to learn how to use an HRM?

The most friendly monitors, the continuous-read ones, are like a speedometer on your car. They require nothing from you but to don it and look at numbers while you are exercising. But I'd encourage you to take the leap and get accustomed to using your HRM as a training tool, a fitness-management device, a stress-reduction instrument, and/or a fat-control aid and not just as a speedometer. If you are committed to training less time and with more intelligence, you'll invest in more features such as a heart zone monitor. If you are committed long term, I'd urge you to invest in a downloadable one. Regardless, buy a book on how to use the information from your monitor and learn everything you can to maximize the benefits of its use.